WRITING
POETRY
in the dark

EDITED BY STEPHANIE M. WYTOVICH

Writing Poetry in the Dark © 2022
editied by Stephanie M. Wytovich

Published by Raw Dog Screaming Press
Bowie, MD

First Edition

Cover Image:
CV Hunt

Book Design: Jennifer Barnes

Printed in the United States of America

ISBN: 978-1-947879-49-2

Library of Congress Control Number:
2022943215

RawDogScreaming.com

Contents

Editor's Note

If you're reading this, welcome!

Writing Poetry in the Dark is a collection of essays that will start discussions and continue discourse about a variety of topics in the poetry community and in those surrounding the craft of writing in the areas of horror, science fiction, and fantasy. I worked hard to make this book accessible and beneficial for all writers and educators at any point in their career, so whether you're just starting out or already a professional in the field, I think there will be something in this book for everyone, and that means fiction and nonfiction writers, too.

It is my belief that poetry is and can be for everyone, and it's my hope that this book serves not only as a guiding light but as an inspirational tool for anyone flirting with the idea of writing a poem or two…or ten. I know as a kid, poetry seemed like this beautiful untouchable artform, and while I was positively enchanted with it, I didn't think it was something that was for me, regardless of how much I read and analyzed countless poets. Sure, I've always considered myself studious, but poetry felt almost elitist at times, like there was a secret handshake I never learned, and as a girl who grew up in a small rural town with a graduating class of less than ninety students, I didn't think poetry existed by or for people like me who maybe didn't have as much world experience or access to resources as others maybe did.

It wasn't until I let my guard down and started experimenting with form and space that I discovered there are many ways to write poetry and that half the battle to doing so was trusting my voice. I learned that while poetry could be ambiguous, academic, or highbrow, it could also be straightforward, queer, feminist, violent, or lush. Sure, it could be serious and steeped in realism, but it could also be satirical, haunting, or cosmic. Better yet, it could be *all of those things at once*. It was in that moment of infinite possibility that I stopped trying to fit poetry in a box of what I thought it was, and instead opened my eyes to what poetry could be.

As I write this, I've been working with Raw Dog Screaming Press for the past 10 years as their Poetry Editor, and I've personally been writing poetry and working in the genre for about 15 years now. Poetry—particularly speculative poetry—holds a special place in my heart, and like most genre writing, I think it exists as a vehicle to not only teach us about the world but to teach us about ourselves all while giving us the space and freedom to work out our fears and dreams in otherworldly, whimsical, and sometimes even (safely) macabre ways. That space for conversation both embraces and breeches the interpersonal distance we might have and need to take on certain topics of conversation to give voice to feelings and emotions that might not be easily conveyed with prose. And yet as I've continued to participate in the community through various editorial relationships, mentorships, and through my own creative work, I've noticed that while there are a ton of craft books out there about poetry, there isn't one specifically aimed toward speculative poetry.

That's where this book comes in.

In an effort to speak to topics such a world-building, magic, dream studies, violence, and mythology, I've worked with a selection of my favorite contemporary poets to build a book that acts as both a resource on craft and an insight into personal process and methodology when it comes to writing the strange and unusual. You'll learn about the intersection of comedy and horror, hear tales from the trenches of collaborative projects, and get about a half dozen or so more books to add to your TBR as you write haiku, practice writing through various POVs, and learn how to create and work with monsters both past and present.

With that said, I hope you'll enjoy this book as much as I enjoyed working on it, and it's my wish that you'll listen to the creative voices inside of you and maybe branch out and try something new or perhaps finish that project that you've had on the backburner for far too long.

Like I said, poetry is for everyone and it's healing and political and versatile and filled with just endless possibilities, so experiment, open your mind, try new things.

You never know what you'll summon in the process.

—Stephanie M. Wytovich, Editor
July 2022

To Sing Dark Songs

Tim Waggoner

I'm not a poet, so why am I writing an introduction to an entire *book* dedicated to the art of writing dark poetry?

I *have* written two books about the craft of writing horror fiction— *Writing in the Dark* and *Writing in the Dark: The Workbook*—and while much of the material in those books can be helpful to horror poets, none of it is specifically geared to their craft. I'm a firm believer that teachers should be professionals in their discipline. I've taught college writing courses for over thirty years, the last couple decades at the same school, and one of the things I learned early on is that *every* English teacher wants to snag a creative writing class. They're sick of grading student essays and long to teach a class that's "fun." The vast majority of these teachers have never published a piece of creative writing in their lives, let alone done so professionally and consistently. So, since I don't write poetry, let alone publish any, I have no experience to pass on when it comes to the genre, which is why I didn't say anything about it in my two *Writing in the Dark* volumes. It did occur to me that a book focused on writing horror poetry would be a wonderful resource, so I mentioned the idea to Raw Dog Press editor Jennifer Barnes in an email one day. I'm not sure what happened after that, but some months later Stephanie emailed to ask if I'd be willing to write an introduction to *Writing Poetry in the Dark*, and I was thrilled to learn the book was in production. I didn't say yes right away, though. Don't get me wrong. I was honored to be asked to write the intro, but I didn't feel qualified. I'd written only one horror poem in my life, and it was rejected by a number of editors. It finally sold when I took out the line breaks and presented it as a piece of flash fiction. So my original impulse was to decline Stephanie's kind invitation, but I took some time to think about it before giving her my answer.

Writing in the Dark was originally the name of my blog, which recently celebrated its tenth anniversary. Without any real plan behind it, I eventually started using *Writing in the Dark* as a kind of branding statement, employing it as the title of my newsletter and my YouTube channel. When I decided it was time to write a book about the art of horror writing, the name seemed perfect for a title too. John Lawson at Raw Dog asked me if they could use the name for a series of writing workshops they wanted to present, and I said sure, and the name became a branding statement for them too. And after they'd published my two books on writing horror fiction, it only made sense to use a version of the name as a branding statement for Stephanie's book. So, I thought, since I'd started the Writing in the Dark brand, maybe that was a good enough qualification for me to write the intro to this book.

Maybe. But it's not as if I haven't had other experiences with poetry, even if I'm not a poet myself.

As an English major, I studied poetry in my undergrad and graduate classes, of course. Much earlier in my teaching career, the creative writing classes I taught were survey courses. These are classes where students explore different genres—fiction, poetry, creative nonfiction, drama—to get experience with them all and decide which one(s) they might like to focus on. And my college used to have three composition courses: One on writing expository essays, one on writing research essays, and one on writing about literature (which of course included poetry). So as a non-poet, how did I approach teaching poetry? I decided that first I should be honest and tell my students I wasn't a poet. But I was a *reader* of poetry, and I knew I could approach the subject as such.

And when I remembered these things, I told Stephanie I'd be happy to write the intro to this book. Not that my writer self isn't fed by poetry as well. I find much inspiration in terms of craft, theme, and style in poetry that I use to make my fiction better. I also like to use lines of poetry for title ideas. And because poems are so often short, many of their techniques can be used to write flash fiction as well. One could make a good argument that prose poems *are* flash fiction and vice versa. And I've written and published a significant amount of flash fiction over the years.

So what do I admire about poetry? What makes it such an effective form for me as both a reader and writer (albeit of fiction)?

There is vast freedom in writing poetry. The subject matter can be 100 percent true, 100 percent fictional, or any combination of the two, and the poet doesn't have to let readers know. Any writing technique can be used in poetry. Want to make your poem a narrative? Go ahead. Want to make it a series of images? Do it. Want to arrange the words in the shape of a star? Awesome. Want to make a political statement? Go for it. Want to make it silly and fun? Bring it on. While poems tend to be shorter than essays or stories, they can be any length, from a few words to an epic hundreds of pages long. They can present clear ideas in plain language, and they can be enigmas to ponder, with many different layers and possible interpretations.

There is an old joke that says a novelist is a failed short story writer, and a short story writer is a failed poet, and I think there's some truth to this. Poetry requires a focus, a precision, a highly developed sense of language, rhythm, and musicality that, while they can and often do appear in fiction, they don't do so in the same ways or to the same degree. Fiction (and nonfiction) can be *poetic*, but they aren't *poetry*.

I don't recall when I first encountered genre poetry—poetry that falls into categories like science fiction, fantasy, horror, etc. I was aware early on in my career that some science fiction magazines published poems, but these were often little more than jokes in verse form, more doggerel than poetry. I do remember some years ago when poets in the Horror Writers Association were lobbying the organization to establish a Bram Stoker Award category for poetry. I wasn't openly disparaging of the idea at the time, but I must admit I was skeptical. I think I'd picked up some literary snobbery in grad school, at least when it came to poetry. Poetry was supposed to be the apex of literary art. How could it fall into the same categories as genre fiction? I decided I needed to educate myself, so I began reading more genre poetry and teaching about it in my classes. Slowly but surely, I began to see how genre-related poetry can be just as powerful as any other type. I suppose that's what gave me the courage to attempt my (so far) one and only horror poem. The strength of dark poetry as an art form is likely already evident to you—else you wouldn't be reading this book—but if it isn't, if you're reading this primarily out of curiosity, I urge you to seek out and read poems from the wonderful contributors to this volume. If you do so, you'll be richly rewarded, not to mention inspired to grab a poisoned pen and try your skeletal hand at some sinister verse of your own (written in bright-red blood, of course).

Stephanie M. Wytovich was the perfect person to create this book. She's an award-winning poet whose deliciously dark writing is as lyrical as it is powerful, and on top of that, she's a wonderful and highly experienced teacher. She's gathered a group of amazing poets to help you start your writing in the dark journey, or—if you've been writing for a while now—to give you some new tools and fresh possibilities for composing scary verse. I wish I'd had a book like this when I was starting out, but I have it now.

And so do you.

So turn the page and let Stephanie and her friends guide you across silent black seas to what Poe called "night's plutonian shore." There you'll see sanity-shaking images visible only in the corners of your eyes, hear disembodied voices whispering blasphemies in languages long dead, breathe cold, fetid air that cuts your throat and lungs like knives of ice. Write down what you experience there—all of it, no matter how strange and unsettling— and return it to the rest of us, so that we might learn to better understand the dark things that reside within us all, and—if we're lucky—make some measure of peace with them.

Return...

And sing.

Dislocating the World

F. J. Bergmann

When we write the weird, we are also writing the familiar. A truly alien entity would almost certainly be unrecognizable and incomprehensible, and it is *comprehension*—up to a point—that induces fear. We can't really process the totally unknown; to give our minds something to chew on—or something to chew on us—a successful horror poem needs to have ordinary elements that anchor the reader to the mundane. Then we can proceed with the dislocating—to generate that sensation of being adrift and alone in an uncanny and frightening strangeness.

Fear is, after all, the essence of horror. "Dark" can mean merely sad or unpleasant; it's necessary to add the outré; the idea, in the reader's mind, that something out of the normal range of existence is out to *get* them or the characters in which they are invested, against which they may have no defense: the poisonous worm in the apple, the malevolent supernatural entity, the mind-control microchip in the vaccine. (NB: your author is fully vaccinated for COVID-19. House Pfizer!)

In short, best results will come from striving for the unexpected.

The Magic Toolbox

Writing poetry in general consists of three elements: prompt or stimulus, content, and technique. These would be 1) what begins the process of writing the poem in the poet's mind, 2) the basic narrative or subject, and 3) how the poem is executed with respect to the writer's tools: form, vocabulary, level of diction, etc.

With regard to prompts, I have found that the *least* useful is to pick a topic to write about, e.g., ghosts, depression, political views, or indeed anything related to the hoped-for effect of the poem. In most cases, your subconscious prefers to grab a sharp-edged rock, a discarded hot-dog bun, a pet on a leash or an infant's stroller, rather than the obvious ball so temptingly proffered, and run. Your mileage may vary, but my most successful poems come from specific constraints that do *not* directly relate to the poem's content; e.g., word lists (there are many ways to generate these, and using vocabulary completely unrelated to the content of the poem will produce striking, memorable work), the challenge of writing in a particular form, incorporating material from another writer, as for instance a first line or a golden shovel, ekphrasis, parody…the list goes on.

One of my own favorite prompts is what I call *transmogrification:* to use the non-trivial vocabulary from someone else's poem in its entirety, in reverse order. An example is my poem "Further" (*The Lovecraft eZine* 38); the source for this poem was "Let Muddy Water Sit and It Grows Clear," a considerably shorter nature poem by Ted Mathys, whose title is reflected in the last two lines: "dwelling where it withdraws to sleep and let the muddy / waters of vacuum clear." The advantage to using others' works is that they force you to expand your vocabulary by using words that may not have previously been part of your normal repertoire. This can be as simple as lifting from an email one of those chunks of bizarre text agglomeration designed to allow spam to clear your junk filter. No, I'm not kidding; two of my long poems that originated from using every word in somewhat excessive spam verbiage are "A Woman of a Certain Age," (*Apex Magazine* 31) where, as I recall, the word "hayseed" triggered all that ensued; and "Maculation," (*Spectral Realms* 10) "…we quarreled / endlessly as to whether their textures / were rugose, slimy, or simultaneously / both," which was nominated for the 2020 Rhysling Award. Having a large selection of interesting words at your disposal is one of your big guns as a poet.

Coming across the perfect title, epigraph, or first line can be all you need to generate a poem that will please you. I found a perfect first line when I heard Denise Duhamel read from the hilarious and highly recommended *237 More Reasons to Have Sex*, and by the end of her performance I was on a roll, already halfway through writing "100 Reasons to Have Sex with an Alien," which placed second in the 2014 SFPA poetry contest and subsequently won the 2015 SFPA Rhysling Award for long poem. My poem "Fame" (*Weird Tales 350*) directly stemmed from the line forming its epigraph, *"somehow managed to attract a small, disturbed following…,"* from Jay Griswold's "Autobiography III," and I could not help but consider what would be my ideal (or most feared) audience. My poem "Avocation" [included at the end of this essay], which appeared in *Asimov's SF*, owes its existence to (and borrows—well, let's be honest, steals) the first line of "Dämmerung" by Simon Armitage: "In later life, I retired from poetry…"

These prompts can also be superimposed: for instance, a first line from whatever political website you're currently perusing, a word that means a shade of green in every stanza, riffing on whatever image appeals to or confuses you from deviantart.com. Maybe make the poem an Elizabethan sonnet, for good measure. I find that constraints like these, more than any other part of my procedure for writing, trigger my subconscious (or, possibly, personal demonic Muse) to produce interesting poems. I do *not* find that obvious horror prompts are any more likely to generate horror poems than those from perfectly mundane sources.

As you mull over whatever prompts you've selected as your jumping-off point (*from high, high on that desolate bridge over a black cascade, the wind keening like an enraged lynx*), a narrative may develop, or just a first—or later—line. Let the content or topic emerge as you write: just begin writing, and subsequent lines will generate themselves by unconscious suggestion from what precedes them. If I get stuck, I find that adding further layers of prompts or restrictions is the most productive approach—apparently the persona of my subconscious is the type of individual who says "Oh yeah? Hold my strawberry daiquiri and watch *this*."

I *do* believe that it's not possible to have true speculative poetry (and horror poetry falls into this category) without at least an implied narrative or story. And in poetry especially, it doesn't need to be a *finished* story: a tantalizing glimpse into a sequence of events that are never fully explained may be far more successful. "End in mystery," Billy Collins advises in *180 More: Extraordinary Poems for Every Day*—and he is right.

Let the Deep Ones Rise

The poems I admire contain ambiguity and duality (or further layers); in general, a successful poem is really about something other than its ostensible subject. Narrative alone (unless it's extremely unusual) is insufficient, as is pure didacticism. By all means let subtexts arise in your work, but I've found that setting out to write a poem with underlying moralization is unwise. This is why seemingly unrelated prompts can be so useful; they allow your subconscious to do what is important without interference, and your poetry will be the richer for it.

I'm a fan of accessibility. I am annoyed by poetry that is so opaque as to be incomprehensible without an introduction or explanation (if you feel that your poem requires an explanation in the submissions cover letter in order to be properly appreciated, rewrite the poem until the explanation is not necessary). While there are specific venues for reactive poems to current events, consider whether your poem will be relevant a few years down the road, or understood on parts of the planet other than the locale where you reside. Poems that can be comprehended by only a select few are not conducive to popularizing poetry or convincing readers or editors to purchase your work.

But I'm also a fan of Easter eggs, to use a software term. By this I mean snippets that can add color to a poem without requiring that the reference be perfectly clear, but yet are still amusing to those with inside knowledge. An example of an Easter egg from "Fame" is "a cold, murky river / whose amphibrachic name began with Y—or was it Z?" An amphibrach is a metrical foot consisting of a stressed syllable between two unstressed syllables; the river that runs through Madison, Wisconsin, my hometown, is the Yahara, pronounced Ya-HAIR-ah. It is also pleasing to me that "amphibrachic" suggests both "amphibious" and "brackish," both words eminently suitable to the context of the poem.

Footnotes are distracting and generally necessary only for especially obscure words (your readers can Google, dammit) or passages in languages other than English. I am all for recreational footnotes, though; see "Night Shift" in *Pedestal Magazine*, which has explanatory footnotes with the mundane origins of all the fantastical flights taken by the poem; e.g., "the twin monoliths of renewal and decay" are in fact the recycling and non-recycling dumpsters.

Wait a Little While

And now we come to execution (*the poem is led out to the stained center of the public square, a thick black hood over its misshapen head*). Note that vocabulary and form are listed as both prompts and techniques, which is not an error. Certain word choices as prompts can drive content and level of diction, to say nothing of meter—but the remaining words in the poem must be chosen by the poet. If a specific form is one of your prompts, then the way in which you satisfy its requirements becomes a matter of technique. But the ultimate goal in your execution should be the unexpected: to take a familiar situation—note that horror tropes themselves (fangs at the throat; a doll whose eyes follow you; pursuit by werebears) can themselves be cozily familiar—and give it a twist; something that the reader won't see coming.

I find it disappointing to read horror poems with clichéd themes and predictable events. Surprise an editor or reader with the unexpected: the damsel *en négligée* menaced by a vampire …who turns out to be allergic to the nightgown's synthetic fabric; a werewolf befriended by a lonely recluse…who decides that dog obedience school is just the thing; a demon secretly wishing for a soul of its own. What can you make from a trope? Better yet, how could you add horror to the most pedestrian parts of your own life: what happens if you use holy water to wash the dishes? Or, as you reach out to switch on the garbage disposal, you hear something in its depths singing in a tiny, shrill voice. Bored with lettuce and tomatoes, you decide to see what happens if you plant the seeds from that little jar you found in the basement…labeled "Dragon's Teeth."

A Stylish Carriage

I don't seem to have a definite personal style when it comes to poetry. I used to think that perhaps this would develop as I matured as a poet, but now that I'm on Social Security and Medicare, I'm no longer expecting some kind of "style" to coalesce. The more poetry (and other writing) I read, the more approaches I want to try—and this is as it should be. The saddest idea I've ever heard expressed by those who want to be writers and artists is that coming into contact with the work of others will somehow taint their work and prevent them from developing their own authentic style. This is a tragic mistake. Neither style nor talent arises from vacuum; the most important thing a poet can do to develop their craft is to read other poets—especially contemporary (i.e., not dead) poets, and not just horror poets. And not just poetry. Listen to spoken-word poets, also—but there is a caveat here: English is not one of the better languages for phonetic spelling. A good dictionary must be your lifelong familiar.

Short-term projects with specific parameters should occur in your writing life as a poet. I've done several collaborations with a marvelous local artist, Kelli Hoppmann, both as ekphrastic poems about her paintings, and with her illustrating my chapbook of conflated fairy-tale poems, *Out of the Black Forest*, written over a period of a few months, which won the inaugural SFPA Elgin Award. A few years later, my compilation of first-contact expedition reports, the SF poetry chapbook *A Catalogue of the Further Suns*, won the Goldline Press award and also won an Elgin. Since these, I've worked on many different projects, all with unique slants and strategies. It's important to keep yourself from going stale; to reinvent yourself every so often. Seek out new tactics that seem intriguing.

Out of the Dead Past

I'm working on a new series of horror prose poems inspired by some of the more unpleasant and distressing, albeit minor, events of my childhood. What I've been doing is taking a recollected scenario and altering it into something more profoundly disturbing; an example from "Eft," inspired by the distressing onset of menstruation: "So when…, after a certain amount of straining and discomfort, as I recall, I discovered a small animal, blood-red and slimed with glutinous membranes, fluttering and squirming in the toilet like some scarlet amphibian variant of a weasel, I flushed it without a word to anyone." For some reason, this approach is not only producing work I'm pleased with as a poet but is emotionally satisfying as well—go figure. Metaphorically, it's like being able to sneak up on the monster from your childhood closet and scare the crap out of it.

I would caution about the therapeutic uses of poetry, however—especially horror poetry. I'm with Alicia Ostriker on this one, who, when questioned on the subject at a reading, said, "Poetry is not therapy. Poetry is *diagnostic*." And I think that those of us who write horror poetry know quite well what we are.

Feeding on the Hivemind

I can't stress enough that you should not write in a vacuum. Writing workshops and critique groups have done more for my own writing than any other process (except reading). Look for groups online or reach out on Craigslist (which is where I found my best writing group, years ago) or social media. Strive to join a group where you are the *worst* writer in the group, and you will benefit the most. While the ideal critique group will support and nurture you, its members should not pull their punches about your work. A group that restricts comments to positive feedback only is not productive.

Note that there will often be situations where interpretations of your work are not at all what you intended, where the lovely foreshadowing you were at such pains to indicate (*the red velvet curtain puddled onto the stage like a gush of blood from a gigantic sacrificial bullock*) is completely misunderstood, or where certain individuals do not enjoy a particular style you favor. Differing perspectives are to be expected; you can cherry-pick what suggestions are useful and discard the rest. Remember that you are under no compulsion (unless your writing group is *very* strange indeed) to take any advice you disagree with or that you feel misses the point—but one caveat: if the group unanimously agrees that something you have written needs changing, they are invariably correct.

Don't become too focused on revision. I do very little revision myself (your mileage may vary), but I wish I had a dollar for every time another workshop participant has said, upon receiving a proposed change, "Oh … that's the way I had it originally." However, as stated above, I strongly recommend running all work by critique groups and beta readers (the latter, preferably fans of poetry rather than family or friends—and, ideally, folks who will have no compunction about giving you negative feedback when needed). And they'll spot the typos and unintended repetitions you missed. I can't stress strongly enough that it's not possible to proofread your own work.

The Castle of Perseverance

Some closing tips for those poets who would like to have their work published (and if you're interested enough in writing horror poetry to buy this book, you're almost certainly also interested in getting it published): much poetry-writing advice places a lot of emphasis on improving your poems to the point where they are "publishable." The dirty secret to publication is that there is no such thing as "unpublishable" poetry: tastes (and competency) vary so much among editors and so many new publications constantly spring up that no matter what you have written (or what is wrong with it), there is likely an editor out there who *will like it*; just keep submitting.

Revising a poem because one editor—or ten editors—rejected it is a waste of your time, unless you are in the unusual situation of having an editor suggest a specific revision with which you agree. Instead, *write more poems*; the quality of one's work improves in direct proportion to the quantity of work written. The poet William Stoddard said he wrote a poem first thing every day; an interviewer once asked him, "What if you can't think of a good poem?" and Stoddard replied, "I lower my standards." Don't let fears about the quality of your work keep you from writing or submitting—*that* would be true horror. Persevere, and write on!

Avocation

first line from "Dämmerung" by Simon Armitage:

In later life, I retired from poetry
to take up the study of magic. After all,
there are only so many ways to use words,
and I didn't care for the modern vocabulary.
Summoning spirits was easy: hadn't the Muses
(a few of them, at least) been at my beck
and call? But other spells were harder to master,
especially those requiring esoteric ingredients.
Nothing in my previous career had prepared me
for reliably identifying genuine murderers' hands
or fat from unbaptized infants, and I'd never
had to write in runes before. Sorcery doesn't
take kindly to rough drafts or revisions.
More than once I fled my dank cellar choking
on sulfurous fumes, covered in violet flames.
Don't even talk to me about succubi!
I grew more and more confused—the fumes,
I expect—and then it was nothing more
than the same old enchantment, in the end.

Writing Speculative Poetry in Experimental Forms

Linda D. Addison

If you search online for "How to write speculative poetry?" you will discover an interesting list of four steps:

- Familiarize yourself with the genre by reading speculative poets and visit speculative poetry magazines online to read centuries-old poems and modern works.
- Identify your subject. Create fantastic poetry inspired by your favorite fairy tale or legend, or simply build a world from your imagination. I would add *favorite nightmare.*
- *Choose a poetic form.* As you craft your stanzas, find a style of verse to match your story.
- Submit your work to a speculative poetry publisher.

Step three is what this section is about: choosing a poetic form. Oh, and there are so many forms to try out—more than I even knew until I started writing this piece.

I love trying various poetry structures, perhaps that is why I teach a poetry workshop where we play with different styles. If you ask online "How many different poetry forms are there?" you'll find sites that mention from 50 to 168 (and growing). You may have heard of types like Haiku, Cinquain, Sonnet, but what about Ars Poetica, Tricube, Concrete?

There are new poetry forms being created, for example in "The Golden Shovel" by Terrance Hayes and inspired by Gwendolyn Brooks, where you take a line(s) from a poem you like, use each word in the line as an end word in your poem in the same order as the original line, and then give credit to the original poet. The title of this poem became the name of a new format.

Why play in the land of forms? Although most of the poetry I write would be considered free verse, I've created poetry in other forms (sonnet, haiku, concrete, fibonacci, etc.). Rather than finding more defined forms constricting, I am inspired by the new, interesting images and music that emerge. These ventures into different shapes and styles haven't dampened my love of free verse; if anything, other forms have added to my poetry toolkit.

A book that opened my mind years ago about writing was *Writing Down the Bones* by Natalie Goldberg. Before reading this book, I pressured myself to make everything I wrote sellable, and then was disappointed when a piece didn't work out. After reading this book and doing the exercises inside, I came to realize that just like physical exercise makes our bodies healthy, I can practice writing, without being concerned with publishing, to make my work stronger. This is another reason to try a new poetic style—to stretch your creative muscles.

Two big influences on my path of investigating experimental forms was meeting Michael R. Collings at a convention and buying his book *The Art and Craft of Poetry*, and then writing a collaborative poetry collection, *Dark Duet*, with Stephen M. Wilson. Collings' book has easy to follow definitions and instructions about different forms and writing with Wilson (who did concrete poetry beautifully) was great fun!

We agreed to throw opening stanzas back and forth, if the receiver didn't feel like playing with that one, then the sender would finish the poem. This was done without judgement or ego. On pieces where we both wanted to play, one would add a stanza, and then send it to the other. Sometimes one of us would write a poem inspired by the other. We allowed each other to edit the collaborative poems as needed. It was a wonderful opportunity for me to dig into the concrete poetry format with Stephen, who was very comfortable in that land. We were both deeply in love with the final book!

Clearly, I can't cover 168 different poetry forms, but let's take a look at a couple of my favorites.

Concrete Poetry

Concrete poetry, also known as shape poetry, is a type of poetry that uses some sort of visual presentation to enhance the effect of the poem on the reader. While the words, writing style, and literary devices all impact the meaning of the poem, the physical shape the poem takes also becomes significant.

This shape can be the whole poem or one or more words in a poem. Some changes you can make to a word to evoke shape include adding spaces, tabs, italics, bold, brackets, dashes, including using any of the symbols on the keyboard, etc. When I teach this in my workshop, there's usually not enough time to work on attendees creating a whole shaped poem, however, we do this form after having created poetry in other forms, and then I suggest each person look at the new poetry for opportunities to enhance it by finding words they can reshape.

Here's an example using the first stanza from my poem, "The Vortex of Damnation" (from *Dark Duet),* which contains concrete elements:

> In the place
>   <between>
> Light and **Dark**
>   innocence dances, unaware
> of the Blood in the future.

Here in the opening stanza of my poem, "Extrication" (from *Dark Duet)*, I break up a word:

> There is a storm, dry and hot,
>   blowing in the edges of my dreams,
> everyone turns to dust, things crawl
>   from their
> s
>   h a
>   t t
>   e r
>   e   d
> organs.

You can decide to shape the whole poem to communicate a concept/image/idea, and the shape doesn't have to relate directly to the words. For example, I wrote a poem, "D2D Candy Corn" for the Halloween issue of *Southwest Review*, and I wanted the shape of the poem to relate to the holiday before I even wrote it. At first, I thought a pumpkin shape would be fun, but I wasn't sure I could do it in a way that would be clear. Then I thought about candy corn and decided that would work by centering the words, even if it wasn't the exact shape.

I daydreamed how I would delineate the three colors in candy corn and considered using italics, regular, and then bold, but I was concerned those choices would take away from the actual poem. A friend, Scott Nicolay, suggested I could use regular text and then separate each level by a line break. I won't go into how the poem content came to be—that's a different discussion about writing!—but the title was the last thing I created because the content of the poem is about a door-to-door salesman.

The thing about concrete poetry is that you have to use items available in your word processor. This includes standard fonts like Times New Roman or Courier, but not actual colors or fancy fonts and sizes, unless you're publishing the work yourself and are willing to spend the extra money to reproduce color, etc.

Although my poem was written after I decided on the shape I wanted, a poem already written in one form could certainly inspire a new shape. For example, if a poem contained images of a river, you could mimic the shape of a river flowing through the poem using tabs/spaces.

It can take extra time and energy to create a concrete poem, or to add shape elements to a poem, but it can be very satisfying and draw readers in.

Take some time to look online for examples of concrete poetry. You'll find some interesting creations you might like to try or that might spark some ideas of your own. The more you play with this form, the more you'll see ways to create captivating work.

Fibonacci Poetry (or The Fib)

This form deeply appeals to the mathematician in me. I first came across the mathematic concept in college as the Fibonacci numbers, often shown as Fn, which create a sequence called the Fibonacci sequence. This is defined as a number that is the sum of the two preceding ones, starting from 0 and 1.

It has a fascinating history, which I won't go into here, but is worth looking up (search online for "Fibonacci sequence in real life"). I fell in love with this in college when my professors talked about how the sequence (also known as the Golden Ratio) could be found in many places such as nature. For example, the number of petals on flowers follow the Fibonacci sequence, and you can see this in lilies, which have three petals, in buttercups, which have five, and in the chicory plant, which has 21. The sequence is also found in the nautilus shell, the spirals of galaxies, and other places in nature and the universe. I've always thought there was something magical about it. It took my breath away when I discovered it was also a poetry form.

In poetry, it's defined by counting syllables. Line 1 is one syllable, Line 2 is one, Line 3 is two syllables, etc. See the chart below, a format I borrowed from Collings' book.

Definition: x = one syllable:
Line 1: x   >>1
Line 2: x   >>1
Line 3: x x   >>1+1=2
Line 4: x x x   >>1+2=3
Line 5: x x x x x   >>2+3=5
Line 6: x x x x x x x x   >>3+5=8
Line 7: x x x x x x x x x x x x x   >>5+8=13

This mathematical progression can go on past Line 7, but you get the idea. The next line is the count of the previous two lines, so Line 8 would be 8 + 13 = 21 syllables. I've not written past Line 8 at this point.

There are several ways to approach this (and other precise forms): use an existing poem and reshape it to fit the line/syllable count, write the poetic prose first and then shape it to the form, or write the poem while counting the syllables at the same time.

Use whatever method works best for you. I usually write a piece of poetic prose, and then create my lines from that, which involves removing words and finding different words—the thesaurus is my best friend—that could fit the image/message I'm creating in the poem.

I've had others say that students enjoy this form because of the counting aspect. The number of syllables per line make an interesting shape, especially if you center the poem. Guess what happens if you create your poem by increasing each line and then start decreasing the syllable count back where you started in the number of syllables? The following is the beginning of my poem "Extrication" (from *Dark Duet)* that I used in the example of concrete poetry, but here, it's been modified into a Fibonacci poem with a few minor changes. After Line 6, I decreased the number of syllables using the sequence rules and then centered the poem. Interesting, yes?

There
is
a storm,
dry and hot
blowing in the edges
of my dreams, the world turns to dust
things crawl from their organs
shattered screams
edged light
crushed
dreams.

Imayo Poetic Form

The imayo is a four-line Japanese form with 12 syllables in each line with a planned caesura (pause) between the first 7 syllables and the last 5 syllables. This form was written to be sung, but that's not required. I've seen the caesura shown with different punctuation such as a dash, a comma, a line break or no visual break between the first 7 syllables and the last 5, so I think you can decide how to best represent that pause (or not).

Definition: x = one syllable; each line is 7, then 5:
Line 1: x x x x x x x   x x x x x
Line 2: x x x x x x x   x x x x x
Line 3: x x x x x x x   x x x x x
Line 4: x x x x x x x   x x x x x

As an example, I used the two poems from above ("The Vortex of Damnation" and "Extrication") as inspiration to create a new poem where the second part of each line isn't directly related to the first part. I ended up with something I really love (in the dark way that I do). This is a new form I tried for this piece, but it won't be the last imayo I write. My tendency is to do a line break for the second part of each line and indent, but I like this version with the em dash or a tab to separate the two parts.

The Vortex

In the Light and Dark of Blood—a storm in my dreams
For each Broken Thing weeping—dry, hot in the edges
The road side thirsts for sweet youth—everyone is dust
Red to stop, green to go, choose—Light whispers, things crawl

In the end, there are several ways to experiment with a form different from what you usually write: whether you start with an image or concept and create a new piece or take an existing poem(s) and reshape it into another style, allow yourself to try something new, to exercise your writing muscles, and enjoy it, much like doing a puzzle.

You might discover another side of your voice to soar or scream with, depending on the slant of your speculative poetry, and in the process create something that you can submit to a publisher.

D2D Candy Corn

(for Scott Nicolay)
He
was bitter
at first, like the
skin ripped from him
by their madness barely

hidden, he should have seen
their Samhainophobia, his mistake
to find an ancient town off the beaten track,
empty streets, old cars in overgrown driveways.
A perfect listener, best sales rep in the state, known
for amusing customers on that holiday with a mask
that glowed in the dark. Certain of convincing people
this old he could customize a plan that would work best,
to maintain the specific lifestyle of their loved ones. A master
at explaining benefits in policies offered. He could outline the

value of each product available, if they hadn't removed his tongue.
He struggled to keep a positive attitude, to make them comfortable,
even as they cut open his skull, thinly slicing his brain to share raw.
Each finger clipped off, each limb removed confirmed to him there
were no deals to close here, no smart strategy useful on the barely
human, ravenous for fresh meat. Life insurance was for the living.

The Art of Speculative Haiku

Christina Sng

I've long been enamored with speculative haiku since I first encountered it in the Science Fiction & Fantasy Poetry Association's official magazine *Star*Line*. Back then, it seemed like a puzzle, a logical puzzle I couldn't unravel. How could so few words tell such an incredible story?

The beauty, I later discovered, was in the brevity of the lines and what's left unsaid for the reader to define.

Speculative haiku or scifaiku encompasses the many genres speculative poetry does: science fiction haiku, horrorku, fairy tale haiku, fantasy ku, and haiku about mythology. It is structurally similar to Modern English Language Haiku, which is very different from the familiar 5-7-5 haiku, defined as counting strictly 17 syllables. Instead, Modern English Language Haiku embraces the traditional Japanese philosophy of writing haiku, which encompasses these guidelines:

- A haiku is typically composed of 1, 2, or 3 lines; containing
- a kigo, defined as a seasonal reference concerning a time and/or place;
- a juxtaposition, two images matching or contrasting each other;
- a eureka, "aha" moment, or a twist in the tale; also
- it's ideally spoken in one breath;
- contains no punctuation except for the em dash; and
- no capitalization except for proper names.

Traditionally, punctuation is not used as it restricts the flow of the poem, which ideally should be read in a single breath. The em dash is an exception as it emphasizes the kigo with a pause. The absence of capitalization, except for proper names, reflects the transient nature of a haiku. It is a captured moment in time and should not be hemmed in by capitalizations that encapsulate it.

A Modern English Language Haiku gives the reader room to imagine long after the piece has been read, and in those short words, it hints that there could be much more to the story. Consider my scifaiku "a world":

a world
of possibilities
my cat in a box

—*Star*Line 39.4*, October 2016

It does not have a fixed syllabic count. In fact, brevity is key, and removing extraneous words makes the haiku stronger. Furthermore, the reference to Schrödinger's cat offers a world of possibilities with a closed box and these are referenced in the first two lines as an idea, then concretely in the final line.

Where is the kigo then? Given this is a scifaiku, and time and place are relative, it would be the moment of space-time when the cat is in the box. Here, the juxtaposition is in the idea of possibilities, first in words, then in an image. More concrete examples of a juxtaposition with two similar images are in the following haiku "a paper plane":

a paper plane
takes to the wind
moon landing

—*Scifaikuest* February 2019

Haiku can be written in 1, 2, or 3 lines. How do we choose? For me, I let the haiku choose. Just as some poems demand to be read in stanzas of 2, 3, or more, a haiku defines its lines when it is written.

One-line haiku, also known as one breath haiku, such that it is read in a single breath, carries much weight in its line.

The key as mentioned before, is brevity. I've always likened writing haiku to chipping away the unnecessary parts of a piece of wood. Similarly, with a haiku, you remove the extraneous parts to preserve the poem. An example of a one-line haiku:

multiverse theory this feeling of déjà vu

—*Sonic Boom 9*, August 2017

While rare in the scifaiku and haiku worlds, two-line haiku do make an appearance.

a leaf on a journey
summer river

—Daily Best, *Haiku University's Haiku Column*, 2021

mesmerized by sunlight
child vampire

—*Scifaikuest*, November 2019

And finally, we reach the classic three-line scifaiku. It is the simplest form to write because there is so much more space to express ourselves.

In the next scifaiku "an eternal divide," the dichotomy of life and death is juxtaposed with the sea and sky, polar aspects of this world that will never meet.

an eternal divide
between sea and sky
the gravity of existence

—Third Place, *Astronomers Without Borders Global Astronomy Month AstroPoetry Contest 2018*

Almost in a rule-breaking close, a lamentation appears snuck into the last line. In haiku, statements are strictly speaking, not allowed. However, the line "the gravity of existence" ties back to gravity's intricate hand in shaping our universe, making it possible for life as we know it, and subsequently, death to occur, and literally separating the sea and sky. Its double entendre gives it further depth by the observation that for us humans, our brief lives weigh heavy on our hearts, knowing death is just around the corner.

The application of the duality of words is a frequently utilized tool in short form poetry. In the next two scifaiku "within sight" and "seeing stars," sight is contrasted with the narrator's final moments. In "within sight," the hope of salvation is seen almost within reach, only to be dashed. The unveiling of what happens after offers the reader much food for thought. While in "seeing stars," one wonders if the narrator is hallucinating after a loss of oxygen. The double meaning in the line "seeing stars" can be read as literal or figurative, and both hold great weight to what appears to be an inevitable end.

within sight
before our engines died
Proxima Centauri

—*Scifaikuest*, May 2019

seeing stars
with my final breaths
hull breach

—*Scifaikuest*, August 2019

Where Modern English Language Haiku defines a haiku as nature-based, another genre of Japanese short form poetry emerges here.

The senryu, which examines the human condition, is embraced within the expansive definition of scifaiku as we, the observers, are often indistinguishable from what we observe.

What other elements make a scifaiku then?

Humor is sprinkled liberally and very much appreciated in scifaiku:

all this rain
stuck in my coffin
all night again

—*Star*Line 44.1*, 2021

The irony of an all-powerful vampire being stuck at home on a rainy night is simply delicious and funny, as are childish antics, even at an intergalactic level, in "android apocalypse":

android apocalypse
they hated us calling them
toaster oven
—*Star*Line 43.3*, 2020

Many poets call the eureka moment the "aha!" moment in a haiku. I like to add a twist to that and call it "the twist in the tale." We strive hard to tell a complete story in a mere few lines, and an effective twist in the third line is the icing on the cake. With scifaiku, we have an entire universe and multiple dimensions and realities to work with. The sky's the limit.

just wanting
to see blue skies again
Arcturus orbit

—*Scifaikuest*, August 2019

It is easy to read the first two lines of "just wanting" and imagining yourself on Earth…until the literal reveal in the third line that you're actually orbiting Arcturus, a red giant 25 times the size of our Sun. A single orbit around Arcturus will take us 25 years. That's a long time to be missing blue skies. Digging deeper, you'll find that Earth-like planets that orbited Arcturus would have suffered a fiery death by now and fallen into the star. Reading the poem with this knowledge makes the reader wonder where and when the narrator saw blue skies. Is the narrator from Earth on a mission to explore Arcturus or an alien with an extraordinarily long life who fled its planet and now orbits the star, presumably for stellar energy? I love imagining the possibilities.

In "snowy plains" below, the twist in the tale is also in the third line:

snowy plains
so hard to hide
a blood trail

—*Scifaikuest*, February 2020

The first line sets the scene. The second makes an unseen observation quickly unearthed in the third, hinting at "death and possible murder," notes *Scifaikuest* editor Teri Santitoro who gave a brief commentary on the horrorku.

I have a formula when conceptualizing this. First, I come up with the kigo. The setting here is a snowy plain. It is day. I ask myself what would contrast the most on this pristine white blanket of snow? What would be hardest to hide? Blood. A long trail of it. I lay the poem down line by line like a layered cake and read it out loud. I remove extraneous words. When it flows in a single breath, it is complete.

Moving further, there is much we can do with this poetic form. One popular option is to make it a joined poem where several scifaiku are connected to form an overarching poem. Each three-line haiku can stand alone but they contribute so much more to the story when they are joined:

Little Red in Haiku

flash of red
through the woods
alarums

old goat
tougher than expected
long lunch

sweetness
of maraschino cherries
baby smells

roleplaying
another species
something new

calmness
tenderizes the meat
grandma not grandma

clear anomalies
the sharpness of teeth
and claws

the speed
of younglings
chest arrow

her sobs
as he fades to black
grandma bones uncovered

—*Star*Line 40.4*, October 2017

By now, you may be asking me: why write scifaiku? My reason is that I love mathematical puzzles and I love brevity: the challenge of reducing a poem to its bare bones within a restricted format, yet telling a complete story.

It is a poetic form you can write on the go: on the train, during grocery shopping, during your lunch hour, while waiting for someone, a moment before bed, on days you feel creatively stuck—the scifaiku is there, ready for you to fill in the blanks and create a full poem.

Plus, the satisfaction you get from completing a poem is magnified by the number of haiku you can produce in a short time. With practice, writing haiku will become second nature.

Back in 2015 when I first discovered scifaiku, I was completely blown away. It was like realizing there was a secret garden in a corner of my backyard. This occured during a time in my life when I was completely depleted. For me, poetry is life. Not being able to write is not living. Scifaikuest was the first magazine I submitted to. My form and structure were completely wrong, but editor Teri Santitoro gently guided me to the right format. If counting syllables intrigued my musical mind, the rules of Modern English Language Haiku fascinated my logical mind. I quickly discovered my favorite poets in this field: Roberta Beary for haiku, Susan Burch for senryu, LeRoy Gorman for scifaiku. Meanwhile, I searched for other venues to submit my growing collection of scifaiku. Many have since found a home in *Star*Line*, the official print journal of the Science Fiction & Fantasy Poetry Association (SFPA) in addition to *Scifaikuest*.

Scifaiku has proved to be such a critical form of poetry that its importance has been cemented in the SFPA creating an award solely for short form poetry called the Dwarf Stars, held annually. The Dwarf Stars anthology contains the best scifaiku of the year. Do pick up a copy from the SFPA. It is always a wonderful read.

How do you start writing scifaiku? Think of scifaiku as a bonsai plant. It is a thing of such beauty, but we cherish it for its minimalism and its perfect shape. As an example, let's start with an idea, an image. Let's imagine an alien octopus in the seas of Titan.

an alien octopus
in the seas of Titan

The first line sets the object of interest and the second gives it a place and time. Now, let's start trimming. First, I remove the "an" since it weighs the poem down. Reading the version below feels lighter and less like a sentence, more like a breath as a haiku is meant to be, bringing the focus sharply on the alien octopus.

alien octopus
in the seas of Titan

At this point, I realize an octopus in Titan would be an alien to us either way, whether we transported it there or it evolved there. As such, remove what is implied. We can remove "an alien" which weighs the scifaiku down.

octopus
in the seas of Titan

Then add something interesting. Often, one single word can offer a whole new world of meaning in a poem. "Octopus" alone looks terribly bare, and although that works, I like to add single words to make a poem more interesting; in this case, I add "purple," which stirs up all kinds of questions as to why an octopus would be purple on Titan.

purple octopus
in the seas of Titan

34

Now we add a twist at the end:

> purple octopus
> in the seas of Titan
> once was us

The last line sparks your interest and sets your gears going by asking how could the octopus (purple no less!) be us? Did it evolve from our DNA? Did a drowning astronaut get eaten by one and turn the alien octopi into a purple one? The possibilities are endless. There are many ways our imagination can take us from here, and that is the essence of a successful scifaiku.

Now look at the images you've painted. Can they be clearer with the addition or removal of a single word? Let's try:

> octopus adrift
> in the turbulent seas of Titan
> once was us

Adding words "adrift" and "turbulent" changes the image of the scene. Now, the octopus is being pulled by the rough, unpredictable seas of Titan and it adds a layer to the final line. This gives our evolved selves a sense of helplessness and provides the poem with greater emotional depth and a greater expanse of time. To keep in line with the brevity I love in poetry, I remove "purple" because the octopus' color no longer matters in the whole scheme of things now that its survival seems to be at stake.

Something I like to do at this point is play around with the line order. There's no hard and fast rule to say the kigo has to be in the first line. Often, it is the last. Let's switch around the lines of our octopus ku to make it interesting:

> once was us
> in the seas of Titan
> purple octopus

Here, I bring back the color of the octopus to focus on the reveal that it is an evolved version of us, and I remove "turbulent" as I find the reveal of the

35

alien octopus the focal point rather than how rough the seas are on Titan. You can read the scifaiku in two ways now:

> once was us
> in the seas of Titan
>
> purple octopus
>
> or
>
> once was us
>
> in the seas of Titan
> purple octopus

Experiment with the line order and the inclusion and exclusion, as well as the replacements of single words, to mold your scifaiku into the final form you want.

Let's try a quick horror example.

> too late—
> mom pulls open the curtains
> I burn

In this scifaiku, "too late" is the kigo and the em dash emphasizes this. You can imagine the shock poor mom will have in the third line but instead of "I burn," let's excise the extraneous "pulls" in line 2 and amend "opens" to "open". Also, let's expand line 3 to paint a more distinct image.

While I go on about brevity, do note that less isn't always better. A clearer image is oftentimes superior.

> too late—
> mom opens the curtains
> I burst into flames

The familiar image of line 2 is juxtaposed against the shocking image of line 3, implying of course, that the narrator is a vampire, and likely, a new one.

Now you try.

1. Start with an idea:

_____ object or kigo
_____ what happens
_____ twist in the tale

2. Excise extraneous words:

_____ object or kigo
_____ what happens
_____ twist in the tale

3. Remove what's implied. Keep your language clear and unequivocal:

_____ object or kigo
_____ what happens
_____ twist in the tale

4. Make it interesting:

_____ object or kigo
_____ what happens
_____ twist in the tale

5. The twist in the tale or moment of enlightenment:

_____ object or kigo
_____ what happens
_____ twist in the tale

6. Consider if you can make your images even clearer:

_____ object or kigo
_____ what happens

_____ twist in the tale

7. Play around with the line order (optional):

_____ twist in the tale
_____ what happens
_____ kigo or object

8. Final edit:

_____
_____
_____

Now write another:

_____ object or kigo
_____ what happens
_____ twist in the tale

_____
_____
_____

Remember, a great haiku is one that gives perfect clarity when you read it, yet its layers of meaning leave you pondering it hours later. I hope you enjoy writing scifaiku wherever you go and may these little nuggets of poetry bring you much joy and delight.

A Slippery World: Writing Poetry About Gender and Sexuality

Lucy A. Snyder

Writing about sex and gender can be a bit sticky. If you grew up in the United States, chances are pretty good that you were exposed to some regressive ideas about human sexuality and reductive ideas about gender. Perhaps you regularly heard "slut" or "gay" (or worse) thrown around as slurs. Perhaps you were raised in a religion that views sex and gender rigidly and trying to navigate their rules as a youth was harrowing. Perhaps your family or community aspired to be more progressive, but nonetheless you grew up being told that sex and sexuality were something to hide, not something to celebrate.

The result? Writing candidly about these subjects can feel pretty risky to a lot of folks. Cis straight poets who grew up soaking in the toxicity of purity culture might feel uncomfortably exposed or vulnerable writing about sex in any detail at all. Sexual assault survivors may understandably find certain subjects painful if not outright panic-inducing. Trans or gay poets who have been forced to closet themselves in bigoted families or hostile communities might have very real worries about outing themselves in their writing, even if they're using a pseudonym. Speculative poets might be concerned that an overt focus on sex or gender will limit their chances of publication.

But these subjects define us as human beings. Gender—regardless of your personal beliefs about its validity, or your frustrations about restrictions and stereotypes inflicted on people trapped in a gender binary—operates in every culture as a framework for viewing people and the world they inhabit. Others' perceptions of a person's gender can be a source of joy for some and a stifling prison for others. Sexuality is deeply tied to desire, love, joy, romance, intimacy, envy, jealousy, companionship, obsession, anxiety, pain, fear, insecurity, and a host of other emotions. Sexuality and gender presentation impact a person's social status, employability, physical safety, etc. They are absolutely core to the human experience, and so they're absolutely suitable subjects for poetry, no matter what that prudish high school English teacher might have told you.

Furthermore, those of us who identify somewhere on the LGBTQIA spectrum may feel absolutely compelled to write about gender and sexuality precisely because so many forces in the world attempt to erase our existence. On August 13, 2021, artist/writer Trung Lê Capecchi-Nguyễn tweeted, "I hate that a common thread among queer folks is like, 'Well, the ins and outs of my sexuality and/or my gender aren't really anybody else's business, but due to compounding moral panics from decade to decade I have to get cozy with oversharing to remind people I'm a person.'"

Is there such a thing as oversharing in poetry? This will depend on the poet, the poem, and the audience the poem is intended for. It's important for every poet to interrogate their reasons for writing poetry. Not just answering the question, "Why do I write poetry?" but the question, "Why am I writing *this* poem, and what do I want it to accomplish?" You can ask and answer those questions at any point in the writing process. It's entirely fine to write poetry that you never intend to show to another soul, just as it's entirely fine to write poetry purely with the intent to sell it someplace. If you're writing just for yourself (perhaps as an exercise in introspection, or to exorcise uncomfortable thoughts, or even simply as a creative outlet) then you can do whatever you like. You're the only one who has to be pleased with how your poem turns out.

But since you're reading this book, I'm going to assume that poetry is not purely a personal activity, and you'd like to share your work with others. I'll further assume that you'd like your work to connect with readers who enjoy horror poetry and other dark speculative genres. Being a poet is certainly not a lucrative profession, but it is possible to sell poems without feeling like you've sold out.

My own take on writing dark poetry is that digging into subjects I find personally uncomfortable, poking at my own fears and psychological scars, is where I find my most powerful inspiration. If something frightens or disturbs me, chances are good that it will be frightening or disturbing to the reader...or I can make it so.

Authors writing in tradition of confessional poets such as Sylvia Plath and Anne Sexton use the personal to make universal observations. I'm not a masochist, and I doubt many other confessional poets are, either. We don't enjoy causing ourselves pain...but the pain is already there, so we have the choice of what to do with it. My own philosophy is that if I have to endure something awful, at least I get to write about it later. I get to own my

40

pain and try to make it useful. Take that raw dark coal and compress it into diamonds. And, frequently, the act of writing about it gets it out of my head. (PSA: writing poetry is not a suitable replacement for trauma counseling. But counseling is also not a replacement for writing poetry.)

It took me years to work up to writing about very personal subjects in my poetry, just as it took years for me to fully come to grips with my own identity as a queer woman. My poetry was *me* in a way that my other writing wasn't. Sharing it in college workshops was terrifying; to my shy self, it felt like I'd decided to stand up in front of class and take off all my clothes. Submitting those poems to editors was nerve-wracking. But as I kept sending my work around, I learned how to distance myself from it. The whole process got easier with time and practice.

So, if the thought of writing very personal poems about sex or gender scares you on some level, that's okay! I'm not advocating that anyone make themselves miserable...but do try exploring your own discomfort. Gently, bit by bit. Push yourself and see what happens. If you find you can't bear to be in that mental space, if you find it isn't inspiring anything useful, don't force yourself to stay. Go do something fun and try something else.

And a key thing here is: you own your experiences...but you don't own others'. Yes, you can absolutely use other people's lives as inspiration. (If you're using events or details that would render an acquaintance recognizable in your work, it's best to get their permission, assuming you care about maintaining a good relationship with them. Lawsuits are a risk, too; see the *New York Times* story "Who Is the Bad Art Friend" for a recent case). You can write from a sexual or gender perspective that is not your own. But you need to get the details right. Don't inadvertently reinforce sexism, transphobia, homophobia, etc. through misrepresentation. Reducing a real, flesh-and-blood person to a fetish, stereotype, a monster, or a punchline isn't a wonderful thing to do.

And those kinds of missteps aren't simply ethical problems. If a critical Tweet or post goes viral, an unlucky poet can find wretched infamy over an ill-advised poem. For instance, *3:AM Magazine* published (and subsequently removed) a poem by Nicholas Rombes titled "jia tolentino." Jia Tolentino is a real person; she's of Filipino descent and is probably 25 years younger than Rombes. She's a former editor at *Jezebel* and a current staff writer at *The New Yorker*. It's unclear that she qualifies as a public figure with regard to laws covering privacy violations, defamation, etc. Regardless, Rombes' poem came off as a weird, icky sex fantasy to many readers. Others also found the poem to be racist and sexist. The lines that people most reacted to are:

Oh Jia

I want to come back
new
into this eely wet
slippery world
with you.

Regardless of the laudable craft aspects of the poem, it was poorly received due to its content, and that poor reception went viral on Twitter. I don't know Rombes, so I know neither why he decided to write that poem, nor how he felt about being mocked and excoriated on Twitter afterward. I do know other people who've received that kind of negative attention on social media, and it was a uniformly awful experience for them.

He probably could have avoided most of that criticism if he'd simply avoided naming Tolentino (or any other real woman) as the object of his narrator's desires. Having made the decision to name her, he could have written a poem in which the "I" didn't seem to be his direct stand-in. If he intended the poem to clearly be the viewpoint of some other man, there were a variety of techniques he could have used, such as writing the poem in third person instead of first, changing details to ensure that the narrator didn't seem to be from Michigan, etc.

But he did name her, and he didn't distance himself from his narrator. And in that context, the poem came off as a fifty-something white male poet sexually objectifying a young, outspokenly feminist woman of color who is more celebrated as a writer than he is. A common manifestation of sexism is reducing a woman's value as a human being to whether or not the man who beholds her finds her sexually consumable or not. It's an attempt to take her down a few pegs. Such an attempt to dismiss a smart, talented woman as either a fuckable decoration or an unfuckable punchline also carries racist undertones when a nonwhite woman is the target. Insecure men will attack or belittle powerful women on the Internet to try to make themselves seem more important, and the poem came off as that kind of harassment. Naming her specifically also gave the poem a distinctly stalkerish air. Another trope the poem played into is that of an older man yearning to reclaim his youth through a liaison with a younger woman, who is treated not as human being but as a magic, virility-restoring amulet. Whether Rombes intended his poem to convey all that or not, that's certainly how it landed for many readers.

3:AM Magazine's male poetry editor deserved some credit for the debacle—after all, he chose that poem as worthy of publication instead of dozens if not hundreds of others—but of course Rombes will have to live with whatever damage this may have done to his confidence or reputation. At least he can serve as a cautionary example for the rest of us.

His poem is certainly not the most sexist poem I have seen in print; it's not even in the Top 20. Horror magazines do not have a particularly good record here, either. Fortunately, the landscape is changing. Editors are more alert to bias (and aware of the need for diverse voices) than they used to be.

But in writing dark poetry, in exploring the grimmer aspects of the human condition, it can be pretty easy to inadvertently play into stereotypes. It's equally easy to write something that comes off as sex-negative, transphobic, homophobic, or misogynistic to another person. And, to be fair, sometimes that's due to inadequate reading skills and not an error in your work. There are people who firmly believe that writing about racism is itself racist, for instance. And for another instance, relatively few people learn how to deeply read a poem before they take university-level English courses. And sometimes not even then. Sometimes the people chosen to be poetry editors at speculative fiction magazines are shockingly uninformed about poetry. You as a writer don't have any control over whether the person reading your poem knows how to read for subtext or understands how layers of meaning can be added through enjambment or symbolic imagery. They might simply be outraged that you dropped an f-bomb or overcome with juvenile delight that you described a penis. This happens.

On the other side of the coin, creators don't actually own every legitimate interpretation of a poem (or other work of art). A personal poem can ultimately mean something very different to a reader than it did to you when you were writing it. It can move their hearts and minds in ways you did not intend but which nonetheless are amazing and valid. This happens, too.

How do you satisfy experienced poetry readers while giving newbies something to enjoy? My own tactic is to ensure that the surface of a poem has a good, accessible shine to it. I tend to write narrative poems, so readers mostly accustomed to fiction get a story. I focus on vivid imagery and enjoy wordplay. While I view the layering-in of meanings in poetry as an artful form of cryptography, a reader's basic understanding and enjoyment of one of my poems doesn't usually hinge on being able to catch the underlying meanings and references. And hopefully experienced readers will find more to puzzle out and enjoy.

The goal for any dark poem is to be *deliberately* horrifying or unsettling. If you're writing about obsession, fear, pain, alienation, or exploring the grotesque, etc. in connection to sexuality or gender, just make sure that the poem is landing where you intend it to for whoever you have chosen as your audience. Be thoughtful and do your research. If you have the slightest concern that your work might come off as unintentionally gross or biased, workshop your poem (or cultivate a group of savvy first readers) and see what others think. You never *have* to revise your work based on a first reader's opinion of it, but at least you won't be caught off-guard if others see your poem in a similar light.

I've covered a lot of things to avoid. So, what are some things to embrace, aside from your first readers and your research?

Embrace form and structure. Look for new ways to write a poem and try out new techniques. Free verse has been in style for decades now, but it's worth learning and using traditional forms. Haikus are popular because they're quick and accessible. But there are specific forms that especially lend themselves to writing about sex and gender.

The first traditional form is the sonnet, which comes from the Italian word sonetto, which means "little song." Most readers have at least a passing familiarity with this type of poem. These 14-line rhyming lyric poems are, literally, made for love. You're probably familiar with Shakespearean sonnets. William Shakespeare famously wrote 154 romantic sonnets during his life, and these are formed by three four-line stanzas followed by a rhyming couplet. Another major sonnet type is the Petrarchan sonnet, which is composed of an eight-line stanza followed by a six-line stanza. Both sonnet types have a volta, a thematic twist or resolution to some type of tension. In the Shakespearean sonnet, it happens in the last two lines, but in the Petrarchan sonnet, it happens at the end of the first stanza or at the start of the second.

There are other hallmarks of these sonnets such as rhyme schemes specific to each type. Further, there are other kinds of sonnets: the Spenserian, Miltonic, terza rima, and curtal sonnets. There's a good article on the requirements and differences at blog.prepscholar.com (do a keyword search on "sonnet"); I encourage you to take a look to learn more.

But the upshot of there being so many different formal styles of sonnets? You, as a poet, can play with the structure however you like. The moment I see a poem that's 14 lines long and deals with love or sex? I know I'm looking at a sonnet. And then I look to see how this sonnet in front of me deviates from traditional sonnet forms. What's the author trying to say through that shift in form? For instance, a deliberately non-rhyming sonnet that otherwise conforms to the Shakespearean form could be literally conveying to the reader that there's no rhyme or reason behind love or attraction.

A second useful form is the sestina, which is a complex poem composed of six stanzas of six lines apiece finished with a three-line stanza that serves as an envoi. Past that, the form gets pretty fiddly; Wikipedia.org actually has a good rundown of the specifics, as does Poets.org. But the upshot is that this 39-line poem involves a lot of very specific and very deliberate repetition of the words at the ends of lines. This repetition lends itself extremely well to subjects involving obsession or anxiety. Sestinas are difficult to write, but if you spend the time on one, chances are good that you'll end up with a solid poem on your hands.

If exploiting that kind of deliberate repetition to explore the obsessive or anxious aspects of love, sex, or romance appeals to you, but 39 lines seems too long? Try a villanelle. This 19-line form is composed of five three-line stanzas (tercets) followed by a four-line stanza (quatrain). Poets.org has a good explanation of the specifics, and Sylvia Plath's "Mad Girl's Love Song" is a classic example. This form began as a type of ballad that didn't have specific rules; its name comes from the Italian word villanella, which refers to a country song or dance. But in the late 1800s English poets took over the villanelle, and the form that resulted relies on a repeated refrain and end-of-line rhyming words. So, it, too is ideal for conveying obsession, anxiety, and madness, but you can take advantage of its roots as a song, certainly. If you wanted to write a poem about people seeking last-chance hookups at a nightclub while Cthulhu's rising, a villanelle might be just your style.

And again: you can pick and choose what aspects of a poetic form you use or don't use. For my unrhymed poem "Cougar," I borrowed the villanelle's 19 lines and a partial refrain as a way to convey the narrator's obsessive thoughts. Think about how form affects meaning and what tradeoffs you might have to make. For instance, sometimes rhyming will come at the expense of style and imagery but will reinforce other aspects of your verses. Do what you think serves your particular poem best.

Beyond structure? Become a regular reader of poetry if you aren't already one; Poets.org is a wonderful free resource. Embrace metaphors and dig deep to find fresh ones. Embrace vivid, sensual imagery if the poem calls for it (and I'm hard-pressed to think of one that won't). Embrace the weird, the disconcerting, the gross. Sex can be odd, ridiculous, terrifying, beautiful, and breathtaking all at the same time. Bring all those things to the page and use them.

Dig deep, and see what slippery, strange, scary, lovely verses you can create.

Cougar

Respect. I got boots older than you, boy,

so don't say the c-word like it's bad.
I know what I'm doing. Do you?
You say you want some sweet young
thing, her head full of fluffy-dovey love,
soft and forgiving. Naive. No rough life
led, no diamond-hard eyes watching
you work. Rosebud beauty just lies
there and sweats while you wish
for a lover who'll bend your pride
to her knee, thrill you and show
you everything they can't capture
on glossy paper or film or electronic
bytes. You can't do better than your own
imagination if your friends all have staples.
My flesh is real, but it's my mind
you want, even if you don't know it yet.

Respect. I got scars older than you, boy.

Wanna see?

Do Not Fear Poetic Collaboration

Jim & Janice Leach

Do not be afraid. You are not (necessarily) betraying your Muse when you craft poems with another wordsmith. The ghost of Emily Dickinson is (probably) not glowering at you disapprovingly. You are not abetting the enemy, compromising your vision, or blunting the power of your work. Unless you are. Trust us, collaboration can even be fun. It can be productive and can expand your skills and your horizons. Though we write horror-poetry collaboratively, our poetic collaboration is not a horror.

For our book 'Til Death: Marriage Poems, we developed a rather extreme method of collaboration, and we lived to tell this tale. We met in high school, married at 19, grew up together, and for nearly four decades we've shared with each other almost every creative word we've written. Even still, we weren't exactly prepared for the high impact, no holds barred form of collaboration we adopted for this particular collection. As we began to assemble poems about the history of our lives together, the horrors and happy ever afters that we've shared as a couple, we realized that the process of our composition could reflect the theme. We could radically collaborate in art as we did in life.

We started slowly, which is good advice for any creative partnership. We respected each other's opinions—even when those opinions were clearly full of crap. In the beginning, we were like a very small, very polite Writer's Group, reading and commenting, noting scansion errors, suggesting a better word here and there, flattering, cajoling.

We were poets on a first date.

Then, together, we dared to cross a line.

It may have first been in "Beta Vulgaris," a clever lyric drafted in a strong voice and persona. The other responded with a substantive revision, clipping lines and massively restructuring thoughts, moving whole stanzas. Or it might have been "Cold Solstice" a sprawling narrative poem that one of us drafted poems which the other plumped with sensuous detail and delectable turns of phrase until the story nearly derailed. Further revisions occurred. And in both cases, a far better poem emerged, one richer than what we could have accomplished with more superficial, flirtatious commentary. We felt we'd crossed a boundary, gone to third base.

We were no longer quite virgins.

We took this step knowing what we were attempting.

Consent in both sex and poetic collaboration is essential.

After that, we went all the way. We took each other's "finished" poems and re-worked them radically. Even odder, we "re-wrote" works that the other had just begun to draft, pieces so new and raw that previously we might have held onto to incubate further because they weren't quite ready for sharing. We have chains of email showing an idea beginning from one of us, acquiring lines and structure from the other, then a radical revision, back and forth. In a sense, some of these poems are epistolary compositions. There are poems in that collection that both of us can ask honestly "Is that one yours? Or mine?" Ownership of individual poems became less important than the effectiveness of the collection.

We also started giving each other assignments, playing Muse. One dared, "Remember that time you made maple syrup. I bet you still haven't forgiven me. Write that poem." The response was "Ostara." Recalling a particularly fierce disagreement, one asked if reconciliation was an option; the other wrote "Apocalypse" in response. We wanted to capture the emotional highs and lows of a long partnership and the effort it takes to stay together. We kept that idea in our minds as we strove to enhance the passion reflected in the poems, not file down the sharp edges. One friend said our book is basically about fighting and fucking and, in a way, that is exactly the vision we wanted to depict: a self-portrait with roses, smiles, and passionate caresses as well as dirty hands, bloody knees, and sweat everywhere.

At times we each felt too vulnerable, that some lines lay too close to our heart strings, that some edits cut too close to the bone. Even after decades of living together, textual intimacy on this level felt risky. We survived partly by keeping boundaries and clearly announcing them. At times, we each thought "I'm only working like this for this collection." And that was fine. At best, collaboration is a temporary arrangement of co-production that stimulates growth in both writers. We emerged better poets on our own as well.

Despite this description of cage-fight collaboration, writing poetry together can actually be great fun.

Poetry is often very personal writing. Some poets find that comments on their poetry land close to their emotions, even when they expect frank and critically worded critiques on other writing they do. We are *not* telling anyone how to feel about their work. It's your own damned poetry after all, which you create for reasons that are nobody's business, and you can adopt any position toward it you want. And still, it is possible for even emotionally entangled poets to collaborate productively when they know what they want, know how to ask for it, and, whenever possible, know how to be gracious with whatever a trusted collaborator offers.

But how does one *become* such a trusted collaborator? Practice saying, "What kind of feedback do you want on this piece right now?" If your partner wants to know "Does this scan?" don't comment that the conceit of the primary metaphor is silly. Collaboration is not an on/off switch; it is a delicate machine with many knobs and inputs. Even though we have radically re-written each other's words in the past, at any given moment while composing any given poem, that interaction needs to be flexible.

We highly recommend the book *Thanks for the Feedback: The Science and Art of Receiving Feedback Well* by Douglas Stone and Sheila Heen where the authors distinguish three different kinds of feedback that actually work: appreciation, coaching, and evaluation.

It's also important to note that there are many different modes of collaboration. We found serial collaboration most effective for *Til Death*. By serial, we mean one of us wrote a piece and the other revised it, with continued back and forth. Due to the length of most poetry, where the whole work can generally "fit" inside someone's head at one time, taking turns seemed to work best.

Be open to other methods if the work suggests it. For instance, Jim has written screenplays with a partner where they drafted an outline together down to the scene breakdown, and then they both wrote a version of that scene as homework, which they read aloud at the next session before composing the scene together, line by line. Similarly, as we write these very paragraphs, we have first cobbled together an outline, written different sections then revised each line together, word by word.

Each collaborator will likely have particular strengths and predilections. For instance, one of us prefers formal and narrative poetry; the other gravitates toward lyrical and image-rich verse. While collaborating, both of us learned some of the other's skills, even though we tended to let the expert work in their favorite capacities.

Collaboration can be a cure for writer's block. We stole this idea from a couple we know who are both painters. When one feels stuck in a piece, they ask their partner to work on it a bit. When they come back to their painting, they literally see new things in it. We feel this is a fantastic use for collaboration. Even if one partner decides to reject all the revisions, the way they see that poem has usually been broken open to reveal new possibilities.

Find a collaborator and steal their jewels.

Note from the emotional poet: protect your subjectivity. Consider keeping some trove of writing outside of your collaboration. We recommend at least a journal or Julia Cameron's "morning pages." *Certainly, collaborate with your whole heart, but know it might be easier if you reserve a pint or two of your lifeblood.*

Many poets, especially at the beginning of their careers, fear betraying their Muse by trusting someone else to help manifest their holy vision. We suspect this trepidation comes from having a clear initial inspiration…that is not particularly complete. The fear is that this idea will get away from them, especially if they let others meddle with its transcription. Spoiler: we've found *all* our inspirations to be "incomplete" until we went through the hard work of hammering them into words.

One way around that fear of betrayal is to practice the craft of collaborating by working with a neutral party's vision, one that is already clear and manifest. How is this possible? Try the poetic equivalent of fan fiction. Find someone who shares a passion for a particular fandom and work on your skills of collaboration by filling in a silent spot in that world. Need examples? The implied sexuality of, say the TOS *Star Trek* gave birth to the Kirk/Spock "slash fiction" of the 70s. Did *Firefly's* Inara study erotic poetry as she trained to be a Companion? A friend of ours, who is by far the most prolific writer we have ever met, composes almost entirely within the universe of the TV show *Glee*. This is a very good time to be passionate about imagined worlds and to find others with that same passion; creating collaboratively in that shared universe could provide an opening, even if the resulting fan poetry is not work that one could publish in the traditional sense. We suggest this technique only to gain comfort with the give and take rhythm of collaboration and the process rather than any specific product.

You don't have to write about your highest aspirations and deepest values with your intimate life partner; you could instead write about your favorite television show with someone you've only met online.

And now for a word from the Writer's Group Marketing Board. Writer's Groups rock. Or at least they can rock. A good group can offer feedback on your work-in-progress from multiple perspectives and can be excellent training grounds for giving and receiving critiques graciously. Writer's Groups abound online and in person, and a meeting can probably be found to fit anyone's schedule. The friendship with other wordsmiths is invaluable, and the networks are priceless. We have had fantastically productive experiences with groups going back for decades. Truly, participating in a Writer's Group at some point in your career is something almost every serious writer owes to themself and their craft.

For good or ill, however, Writer's Groups are perhaps the speed dating version of collaboration. In the context of a meeting, it is difficult to get much more than superficial feedback. That critique will often also be of varying quality since members will range in skill level and expertise, perhaps even less than you. Worse, sometimes skilled commenters can have non-charitable views of the very genre one writes. It is best, it goes without saying, to collaborate with someone who views your writing with respect.

An anecdote? We were in a group 30 years ago that met in a drafty old Baptist church. One of the few members who wrote poetry insisted that her poetry was literally directly dictated from God. When we did a group reading, she prefaced her poems with the phrase "this is a poem the Lord gave me." Needless to say, with such a divine collaborator she was not open to the group's feedback.

Writer's Groups also have acute liabilities especially for writers of speculative poetry. In most groups we've experienced, it is common to find writers who work in different forms: poetry, short story, even nonfiction prose. We have both shared poems that ended up in *Til Death* with Writer's Groups who focused entirely on poetry, only to receive cold uncomprehending stares. We attempted to explain speculative literature and got as response "Oh, like Edgar Allan Poe?" Such feedback, let's say, was less than transformative. We have great hope that it is easier to connect with other speculative poets online, and we have not yet experienced much success making those connections. We have a handful of trusted readers, scattered across the globe, who seem to get what we do and who serve as our first readers. At present we don't have a group. Writer's Groups can be incredible…and it's best if they can give feedback deeper than grammatical or spelling corrections.

In "Who Goes First," a poem we wrote [specifically] for *Writing Poetry in the Dark*, we've mimicked a dialog. Two voices tease and answer, mourn and mock each other. We play with verb tense, with verb modes and verb moods. The placement on the page casts the poem in two voices; however, that is artifice. Both voices are both of us. The conceit of the poem enhances the sense of play and competing agendas. The composition of this poem represents our goal of collaborative writing. We began with a conversation separate from writing—a would-this-work kernel of a poem. The nugget. The hook. One of us –does it matter which?—gave the work a working title, which of course casts a shape for a poem. A few drafted lines set a mood and tone. The other of us slipped inside the poem, stretching and pushing, playing with the what ifs and why nots. And so on. An exchange of words and ideas on this level makes a poetic string of words into threads; together we weave something bigger, whole.

Something that fits us both.

In conclusion, fear not. Collaboration need not be a horror show.

We, at least, survived to tell this tale.

Who Goes First

"If one of us dies, I'm moving to Florida" —Midwest Folk Wisdom

If you are first to break our vows,
And settle into that narrow bed,
The cold one that allows no partners
                    I'd curl alone beneath our stack of covers,
                         No other body to warm my limbs,
                           No orbit drawing me near.
I might drink my dinners,
purchase groceries at the package liquor downtown,
A square meal in round bottles.
                    I might prepare your favorite dishes,
                      Savour memories on my tongue,
                        Peppering forkfuls with tears.
I'd put up a Christmas tree just to spite you,
Perform the household rites in new ways,
Daily smudge the tiles clean.
                  I will slam the doors, crack the windows,
                    Creak the floors, paint the walls pink,
                      Decorate in floral chintz.
The rooms might grow too loud, crowded with memories,
So I'll empty the excess to leave
Bare walls and cello waiting against a single chair.
                  I'll recall the resonate thoracic ache,
                    your music hallowing my chest,
            Her wooden neck caressed against your shoulder.

Like Adam reversed, robbed of my Eve, I name all the animals as pets
Chickens, dogs, birds that will shit on the sofa, cats that will eat the plants,
Rabbits that enrich the soil with each dropping.
                  My one long-haired fat lap cat
                  Spoiled with treats and delicacies
                  My hands buried in his rumbling fur.

I'll dig memories out of the garden.
No more broccoli or herbs.
Or I will never garden again.
                    Let it fallow, go to weeds, to deciduous forest.
                        Or instead grow only persnickety roses,
                            Propagate your namesake variety.

I will systematically bed all the widow-gardeners in the neighborhood.

                            Please. At least wash your hands.

All the ways we haunt will fill volumes.

Here Are the Stairs to the Dark Cellar; Yes, You Must Go There: POV in Dark Poetry

Timons Esaias

Initial Threats

Point of view—POV—is something we are trained to suppress, or at least to deliberately restrain.

We are raised to be polite, and raised to be factual, and raised to keep our distance, and none of these are useful traits if you're writing dark poetry. What is needed is to unbuckle the seatbelts, turn off the airbags, strip the insulation off the wires, and grab hold. If you were taught that adopting an imaginary point of view in poetry is an error, this essay is meant to break you of that belief.

POV is a primary tool in our toolkit. It is the essence of our project. Indeed, the readers of dark speculative poetry—often reading for courage—*want* you to go someplace transgressive. They want to see *inside* the darkness, *inside* the victims, *inside* the monsters. Yes, you must go there.

"How do I do this?" you ask, from under your rock. Well, you do it by adopting the full range of POV possibilities open to prose fiction writers. But before I give some examples, let me warn you about two sinkholes that block our path.

Sinkhole #1: The poetry world is vast, and most of us only experience part of its range. Many of you will have been taught by and surrounded by Objectivist poets, who treat poetry as a form of non-fiction. Poets, they say, observe the world, report on it accurately, and then—sometimes—suggest some meaning. That is a noble discipline but is a trap for the dark/speculative poet. Yes, a clinical approach can make horror seem more inevitable, but most dark poetry is a work of the imagination. Your readers are wanting things to be *worse* than the merely real. Real they can get on the news.

Sinkhole #2: Another major movement in modern poetry can confuse the dark poet, namely the Confessional discipline. This poetry asks you to look inside, and into your past, and put some painful stuff on the page. It must be accurate, or you're cheating. Only dark poets who are also serial killers or organ-snatchers will benefit from this approach. You may have encountered poets who tell you that you *can't* write about imaginary characters, you *can't* make up a persona, you *can't* write about fictional monsters, races, or victims. Ahem. Yes, you can. Indeed, dark poets, you must.

Edgar Allan Poe, the Ur-practitioner of dark poetry, set the standard for use of a fictional point of view in both his prose and poetry. He preferred to use a first-person POV, and those first persons were fictional. Poe might have embraced the Confessional discipline, but he would likely have insisted the confessions be fictional, magical, even supernatural.

His is the path that most dark spec poetry now follows.

There are monsters and ghouls on each side of this path, vampires hovering above, and shapeless monstrosities tunneling just below the surface. Good. This is how it should be.

As I said before, we need to embrace the full range of POVs that are open to prose fiction writers. Let me discuss three recent examples, each illustrating a different POV technique. And we'll begin with America's favorite choice for anything: All of the above.

Example A: For an illustration of Omniscient POV with In-and-Out, I'll address Marge Simon's "April Moon," which originally appeared in *Bete Noire*, 2017. It's a modern story about a sixteen-year-old Diana who has magic powers, probably connected to the Moon, and who gets raped. This is dark material indeed.

The poem starts with Exterior POV but slips into internal Diana by the end of the first stanza.

She turns sixteen,
sneaks out of the house alone
in her brand-new skinny skirt and boots
feeling like she owns the April moon

The third stanza shifts to the viewpoint of the cop who finds her on the side of the road and takes her home. So yes, poetry can use the techniques of multiple POV!

The poem then shifts back to Diana's perspective, and we learn about the corpses of those five boys, and Diana's choice to leave town. The last two stanzas are back in Exterior Omniscient, letting us know that the abusive father is lucky he never tracked her down.

I chose to break down this poem first because it makes several key points:

- You can tell an entire story, from inciting episode to resolution, in a single poem.
- You can use multiple points of view, both Interior and Exterior, in poetry.
- One should not forget that some narrative power can come from what didn't happen, as well as what did. By withholding the detail of what happened to the boys until the second half of the piece, it redirects the story we're expecting to be told. The character transforms for us, while at the same time we're being told about the boys transforming, perhaps, into stags.
- In sum, poetry may be shorter and simpler than prose, but poetry can still use all the techniques of prose storytelling.

Example B: Next there's "Tatiana" by Mary Turzillo, which first appeared (2012) in the Dark Regions Press collection *Lovers & Killers*, and which appears alongside "April Moon" in Simon & Turzillo's new collection, *Victims*.

This poem is a bit longer than the first, in six long stanzas. Tatiana is a tiger in a zoo, and the poem combines Omniscient opening lines ("Tatiana understands human words.") with Interior POV thoughts ("Did the sister eat the cameraman? / Was his liver fat and tender?"). This device puts us mostly in the tiger (without being eaten first) but allows some additional information in at the same time.

Here's the first stanza:

Tatiana understands human words.
While she grooms her whiskers of blood
she listens intently
if imperfectly
to the gossiping keepers
how an old tiger was found dead and dissected
in a zoo in China,
the cubs stillborn and in a freezer,
how another sister ripped out the bowels of a keeper

formerly beloved
who said the wrong thing, moved too fast,
moved too slow.
How a tiger, little older than a cub,
was found fettered by a bicycle chain
along route 18
shot five times in the head.
Tatiana understands.

As an aside, a nice trick one can use more easily in poetry than in prose is illustrated by this poem. There is a repeated structure in the stanzas (The stanzas begin with what Tatiana understands: gravity; boys; space, and air; blood and softness and slow ineffectual prey. Except the last, which tells us what Tatiana doesn't understand.), and this repetition has the effect of justifying the technique. The poet may not have convinced the reader that their approach is valid by the end of the first stanza. But by repeating it again in the second, you say, "See? It's a *thing*." The reader can then be sucked in, and by the third time they succumb, as though you had revealed a Law of the Universe.

This poem also uses Omniscient POV with In-and-Out, but this time it's only for a single character's Interior POV.

Example C: Sara Tantlinger's Bram Stoker Award- and IHBA Award-winning collection *The Devil's Dreamland: Poetry inspired by H. H. Holmes* is a study in POV in dark poetry. I have plucked "Dark Appetites" from the seething cauldron of possibilities because it goes inside the mind of a serial killer, H. H. Holmes himself. It begins:

Myrta does not live here anymore
second wife, second baby,
I will keep them alive
but away from me
I will keep my spawn
out of curiosity

This poem, five stanzas, uses strict Interior first-person POV. A reader who picks up a book of poems about a serial killer's rampage is probably wondering—among other things—what the killer is thinking, what he was like on the inside. If you listen to the Objectivists or the Confessionalists, you won't be able to answer that question. If you're willing to employ the magical powers of POV, you can at least seem to go there.

Tactical Note about Pronouns

While I'm discussing POV in poetry, let me mention a tactical trick. The trick starts with: pronouns. They're a problem. Confessional poets often drag a great burden of I's down the page. *I this, I that,* and *then I thus,* and *then I so.*

Instead of being Interior and engaging, all those personal pronouns can drive the audience out of the dream that the poem should be evoking. The same is true with third person Interior if it ends up all *she this* and *he that* and a pronoun in every line. It doesn't matter that the images come through the brain or the eye of the imagined character; the pronouns are pushing the reader outside.

The solution is to simply drop as many of the pronouns as you can. Poetry doesn't require meticulous grammar, after all. I thought this thought / had that opinion / wrote six lines to you / hoping a heart would change / knew the maggots / had gotten there first. (Six lines, one pronoun subject, one pronoun object.)

Now if you're writing *Exterior* POV, the reverse can be a useful tactic. Use the character pronoun for anaphoric emphasis:

For I will consider my Cat Jeoffry.
For he is the servant of the Living God duly and daily serving him.
For at the first glance of the glory of God in the East he worships in his way.
For this is done by wreathing his body seven times round with elegant quickness.
For then he leaps up to catch the musk, which is the blessing of God upon his prayer.
For he rolls upon prank to work it in.
For having done duty and received blessing he begins to consider himself.
For this he performs in ten degrees.
For first he looks upon his forepaws to see if they are clean.
For secondly he kicks up behind to clear away there.
For thirdly he works it upon stretch with the forepaws extended.
For fourthly he sharpens his paws by wood.

For fifthly he washes himself.
For sixthly he rolls upon wash.
For seventhly he fleas himself, that he may not be interrupted upon the beat.
For eighthly he rubs himself against a post.
For ninthly he looks up for his instructions.
For tenthly he goes in quest of food.

The repeated pronouns (and, in this case, prepositions) can become legal propositions, or commandments. When the person or monster in your poem is fictitious, this insistence on its existence—pronoun after pronoun—forces the reader to believe.

In Sum

Returning, then, to my theme, point of view is your entry wedge into better writing. If you write to amuse yourself, or to challenge yourself, then putting yourself (and thus, the reader) into the various dark points of view can be magical.

If you are writing for catharsis, even better. Put yourself in the evil place, the place where the pain resides, the place where the evil, the indifference, the cold comes from. Sit down in front of the oncoming train, while not actually doing anything of the kind. Catharsis is there. Healing is there.

Power is there.

Author example: The following poem [published long ago, in *Edgar: Digested Verse*] uses second person, but is actually from the POV of a frustrated instructor.

Horror 01

The true adept is unmoved; calm,
utters a terrifying chuckle
from under the bed, or a scream
from behind the closet door
but remains unmoved.

Good.

Now slip out and advance, remorselessly,
upon the terrified victim.
Slowly, good, remaining calm,
unmoved, hunting without passion,
without exhilaration.

Good.

Now dangle one talon before the eyes.
It paralyzes, but we remain unmoved,
calm. And now the evisceration,
a single stroke, calmly,
I said…that's not the way at all.

Spoiled.

Dramatic use of intestines, yes,
but tomorrow we must begin again.

World-Building...in a *Poem?*

Albert Wendland

World-building takes time and space.

But in a poem you have little of either.

Writers of big baggy novels can indulge themselves and use methods similar to those in writing a first draft, either "planning" or "pantsing" their world, outlining ahead or diving into it by instinct. In the first case, the building is done early (astronomy and geology, sociology and economics, psychology and individual motivation, characteristics of the science or magic) and is sometimes completed even before writing a word of the story. Or, in the second case, one can plunge in and make it up while going along, hoping that it all makes sense and will hang together after being completed.

Of the two methods, planning is safer. Your world is already complete, and you can easily place your story into it, using all the many details you have ready in your voluminous notes. But the problem with this method is that it can become *too* fascinating, and you get so sucked up in creating the world that writing the book can be delayed and grow less interesting. You lose yourself—and your time and enthusiasm—in the minutiae of fleshing out the background.

On the other hand, with pantsing, you can start immediately, jump into your story at the moment inspiration grabs you. Then, as you go along, you drop in the necessary aspects of your world by creating them on the fly—or, more lazily, include bracketed comments like "add economic trade rules here" and just keep going. You put off all problems until later because you're just too busy scripting, and you don't want anything to get in your way.

But this method is dangerous. You can lead yourself quickly into contradictions, unrealistic and unfounded claims, details that, in the end, just don't add up. You then might have to rewrite the whole book because not until now, after completing it, have you learned what your world *really* needs.

As for poetry, given the average length of a poem (let's assume you're not writing one as long as a novel or even a short story), you might think the second method would work best. But both approaches are just as useful, even in a poem. They simply get applied differently and are used in special ways. Also, readers are usually more understanding of just how limited a poem can be in creating a self-contained world. It *is* poetry, after all, where the *suggestion* is everything, the hint, the image that leads to wider associations outside the poem.

If the goal of a novel is to define a world and thus contain it, the function of a poem is to allude to that world and thus *illuminate* it in bursts of light (or of *in*sight, the perceptive understanding or creativity that a reader brings to the poem). A novel's world is lit in the steady and studious glow of a lecture hall. But a poem's world is a dark landscape seen in tantalizing flashes of lightning, inspiring the readers (or "electrifying" them) more than rationally explaining to them. A novel has room to create an ocean on an alien planet through maps, specific composition, exact depths, precise age, in a full and logical exploration of it. But a poem suggests an ocean by splashing water into the reader's face, shooting out sensory glimpses of taste, smell, wetness, cold.

If a novel defines and contains, a poem implies, intimates.

Using One's Own Created World

As in all speculative poetry, every word must count. Space is limited and attention span brief (you can't afford the indulgence of the escalating tension of novel storytelling). Knowledge of the world needs to be telescoped and immediate—the backgrounds impressionist, the brushstrokes fast, evocative, open-ended.

If your poetry lies within an SF or fantasy world that you've already created (as so much of Tolkien's poetry is), and if the world is known enough to your readers, then you can do much with just quick references, "name-dropping," and take full advantage of any planning form of world-building you've done before. Let's say a fictional universe involves background alien races called (in my own created future) the Airafane and the Moyocks, and they once inhabited the early galaxy but eventually warred against each other and became extinct. Any reader who has read my novels would recognize them.

But for non-readers of the books, quick associations in the descriptive words applied to the names are then necessary. Yet this doesn't have to go much further than "ancient" and "extinct" for the races. Words in poetry are meant to imply associations more than just pin down identity, serving double duty so that even a non-series reader can get the point. For example (all poems are from the author's *Temporary Planets for Transitory Days*):

> Here, on our planet...
> Where Airafane walked
> And Moyocks prowled,
> Where fallen are the mighty,
> Where legacy cities
> No longer stand.
> ("Barinda's Tale")

Not much background history is given, but the references hint at, if only slightly, a tragedy that occurred between the two cultures. These small allusions, presented in quick time, encourage the reader to open the poem to wider connections—and they then can reference *any* pair of civilizations caught in a trap of possible aggression, loss, and regret. The greater details of the created world's history thus need only be implied.

The Worlds of Others, Real or Created

If you don't have a created background of your own, you can still refer to outside and already known real or created worlds. Here too, just a few words are enough to bring in realms of scientific discovery, *Dracula*'s Transylvania, or the brutal threat of Lovecraft's universe.

For example, NASA space probes have supplied bountiful details about the other planets of our Solar System, and most readers of speculative poetry would be familiar with them, as in:

> Jupiters like agates, jaspers like Mars,
> The snowflake obsidian of Pluto's surface,
> The aquamarine of cloud-faced Uranus.
> ("Litanies of Worlds")

The association with semi-precious gems suggests the "collecting" of planets, the treating of them like precious finds that we then possess, or store in vaults, or show off on shelves, or make into commodities. These images lead to the ultimate question in the poem: what will we *do* with these other worlds once we reach them? "Will we consume, / Or will we savor?" The accurate details (the planets really do resemble these stones) thus suggest a theme and raise its question.

Science now knows worlds of even other stellar systems, putting us in that wonderfully creative realm where what we understand is small and so ambiguous that room is left for interpretive embellishment. For instance, we believe some exoplanets might have different types of rain based on substances besides water—glass, methane, sulfuric acid, iron, diamonds (even sapphires and rubies). What would that be like? What if you actually stood there within it? Novels can deal with the problems of survival (which would be drastic) while poems can spin off on whimsical wonders or shocks of horror. The potential behind any such speculative knowledge is food for poetry.

Some already created worlds are so much a part of our common culture that they too can be tapped. We don't need to explain the associations that come with such words as "elf," "fairy," "troll," "dragon," "T-rex," "raptor," "wizard," "witch," "demon," "ghost," "werewolf," and "vampire." Indeed, given that we have all the stories of mythology and folklore to pick from, the trick is more to avoid the standard associations, so many of which have become clichés, and to come up with new takes on them. A whole planet's worth of mythology exists, beyond the over-used European stories—like Bushongo, Mbuti, Maasai, Berber, Malagasy, Zulu, Yoruba, Palo, Scythian, Ainu, Qiang, Romani, Hittite, Ossetian, Papuan, Lakotan, Olmec, and Mapuche—to mention just a few.

Works like *Frankenstein* and *Nosferatu*, SF movies of the 50s, the classic books of Verne and Wells, have saturated popular culture in so many ways that they've taken on shared consensus "realities" of their own, and can stand a metaphorical name-drop or two. Though the question of "fair use" in poetry is just as legitimate as in prose, a poem's similes and references are brief, and used more for elucidation of the subject than exploitation of the object, focusing on the "tenor" rather than the "vehicle."

Many "worlds" are thus available, already out there and part of the public mind. In the same way that every word in a poem must count, each reference must do the same. And such references to known settings—not long descriptions and often just titles or names—can open up broad realms of association.

Using Images to Break the Frame

The limits of poetry are also its advantages. The need to work within confining structures, short spaces, rigorous formats, and a set rhythm or pattern of rhyme, forces images to perform many tasks, to suggest and embellish as well as identify. Any image can thus become a spotlight that illuminates concepts either existing or spontaneously created outside the poem. The abundance of overtone or connotation in such pictures can thus break the poem's confining frame, deconstructing basic structures while maintaining them. It's like the pantsing in the other mode of world-building, the off-the-cuff creation that occurs as much with the reader as it does with the writer.

In many ways, the limits of the poem are almost intended to break down, to be pushed aside by the swelling impressions the words lead the reader to experience. Though this cracking of the frame is almost planned, the resulting creation of something outside the poem is caused as much by the reaction of the reader. This makes the reader not just a participant but another pantser, adding to this form of world-building.

For example, the two following fragments of a longer poem (called "Nomads in Love") were meant to stay within a three-line structure (not quite haiku since the syllables weren't counted). The planned—or hoped-for—impression was a sense of transience and travel, of moving from one planet or landscape to another and never lasting anywhere long. But the "nomads" are not frightened or saddened by such brevity, so a summary suggestion of acceptance and enjoyment is needed:

Sites passed,
Travelers ways,
Temporary planets for transitory days.
   ("Nomads In Love")

The last line is an attempt to break the frame of the poem (its longer length helped), to open up both the lines and the reader to greater associations—and to make a memorably rhythmic line. The "planets" can be taken as both literal and suggestive, as locations and travelers not quite defined but left open, producing a resonance in the reader beyond just the identified. If the rhyme provides closure, the phrases are meant to hint at something more uncontained, a possible delight in the brevity of both place and time.

In a similar fragment from the same poem, a style of dress becomes mood, a person transforms into landscape, and desire connects the intellectual history of Romanticism to a widening emotional space:

> Gems moon-white, dress dark blue,
> It's Romantic twilight,
> Or the landscape of you.
>   ("Nomads In Love")

In all such lines, a poet can take advantage of the poem's ability to transcend its structure through its images, to contain something bigger in a narrow cage and then to let the reader open that cage, for the image to possibly fly again, to lead the reader into a new world—of moon, twilight, color, and desire, felt for both a person and a place.

Stacking the Images

Another way of signifying a built (or yet building) world is to bury the reader in new imagery, pouring into the lines as much as possible. And each image or reference doesn't need to be explained or fully "shown" (if a little outlandish it might even add to the effect). The example below attempts to mirror the wildly creative imagery of early SF comic books (when the space program was just getting started) and their mood of wonder at what might be found in space. A list of such alien wonders is presented in abundance, suggesting a rich universe alive and crowded with fanciful objects. The number of images becomes more important than their clarity or plausibility, as in:

> Jungle planets where tree-trunks sing,
> Egg moons in nests of debris,
> Worlds with targets, octopi clouds,
> Globes with hoops and internal dynamos...
> Orbs alive, rhomboid, square,
> Rocks that leer or flowers that dance,
> Searchlight fish with fruit-like eyes,
> Violet gazelles under lemon skies
> Chasing fugitive owls of soft lime-green.
>   ("Litanies of Worlds")

The naiveté of some of the images (like square worlds) is meant to suggest the childlike fascination in the early attitudes toward space travel, a quick creative pantsing leap into a wealth of marvels unrestrained by science and realism.

This stacking can be used for the opposite feeling too (demonstrating the method's effectiveness), showing the fears from the same Cold-War period that darkened, and in some ways generated, the space program itself. The many invasion-of-space stories were just as unrealistic, but they implied the terror that touching the night sky might bring retaliation instead of wonder, might inform the universe of where we are and attract terrors that would plummet onto blissful 50s culture:

> Flying saucers over chopped-up buildings,
> Derricks and forklifts reaching down from above,
> Waters rushing into the streets, frogs invading,
> Colored ray-blasts seen even in daylight,
> Chromium Chrysler Buildings with holes,
> Aliens tearing up suburbs built by Frank Lloyd Wright,
> Snipers competing in armies of the future
> With hovering belligerents of cosmic terror....
> ("Crashing Suns")

This stacking of images is like pantsing because it throws in concepts as they come to mind, building a quick collage of impressions. That they're inconsistent or contradictory doesn't matter since the brewing of responses in the reader is the point, the cavalcade of sensory images making the reader feel inundated— producing a sense of apocalypse, the smashing of deluded historical placidity.

Not the Thing, but the Perception of the Thing

An interesting aspect of prose SF is how new and unseen objects are described. Since they've never been encountered in reality (we can't get close enough to see the direct effects of a black hole, the true colors in the swirls of nebulae, or the discharge from postulated iron volcanoes), the depiction of these objects is mostly imaginary. And even though we can base them on scientific data, we can never declare with certainty the small sensory details in perceiving them (like just how green the sky would be if an atmosphere had chlorine in it).

So to express the alienness of the sight, writers will sometimes avoid describing the object and instead give the *reaction* to it, the observer's response of frustration, pleasure, awe, or confusion. And poetry affords an ideal place where these methods can be highlighted—by using the stacking method described before. This tool is applied in the following lines, which attempt to suggest how it would "feel" to land on an alien world and see it for the first time. No specific objects are given, just the sensory, creative, and emotional *responses*:

> Your brain uncouples like an unleashed drone...
> Colors grow and become unruly...
> Details call for equal attention,
> Old standards of perception dissolve,
> Order tilts and is made vertiginous...
> Input's a landslide, nothing's subordinate...
> You're radically lost in destroyed definitions,
> You exceed experience, your clarity melts.
>   ("First Light")

Poetry can punch out many such examples of dislocated understanding, of details becoming "unruly," of making "vertiginous" standard means of perception (like categorization, or the judging of distance through the fading of objects), of rejecting a hierarchy of importance—all to make the reader feel invaded by the "not-you."

Unlike a novel which has the room to conceptualize the landscape in a rational frame, a poem can speak directly to how a human can be absorbed by the scene, immediately possessed by it. This amassing of conceptual notions is like the stacking of visual images, but a lack of precision is emphasized instead, the moments prior to apprehension, when identification is still on the edge ("Is that a tree? a rock? a bird? a cloud?"), still in a state of mystery that's baffled and unhinged.

Poetry, with its fragmentary or bolt-of-lightning immediacy, again breaks through its confined structure. Alienness is built not through the object but through the struggles of the subject, the human mind struggling to "see."

Mood, Memory, Reaction, Feeling

Talking about perception and its limits can be *intellectual*, a pondering of how new things could be taken in. The stacking of images and the referring to outside worlds are *structural* moves, part of the plan, to convey impressions that are sensory or disjointed. But in all these cases, the ultimate point is to produce an *emotional* response in a reader. This happens in all these methods, but the direct use of feelings, whether suggested or stated outright, encourages the reactions even more. And again, poetry has the advantage.

For example, one reason for horror poetry's popularity is its immediate and open appeal to the emotions. The hint of the uncanny, the subtle infusion of the unknown, the shock of a sudden threat—all these find effective delivery in the knuckle-punch or needle-prick or creepy spider-web feathering of a poem. For SF and fantasy, when a fully created cosmos can be referred to in just a few words, the poet can aim for the one image, recollection, or reference of that other world that will strike straight to the feelings of the reader—to the wonder, awe, loss, longing, or fear of the unknown.

In the following example, a scenario is placed so far in the future that the Earth is almost forgotten, neglected and misplaced. But we don't need the details of what's happened, just a few consecutive images:

> One time soggy wet rag of a world,
> Ice-caps melted, animals extinct…
> We debated whether to insulate you,
> Preserve you inside a silver globe
> With memories projected on the inside screens,
> Your histories displayed, your stories retold,
> In a vast running playhouse for the stars.
>   ("A Song of Distant Earth")

Preserving the Earth in a silver globe with running theater on the inside, like a movie screen, would be a large-scale conceptual topic in a novel—and surely not survive the rigors of hard SF. But in a poem it's more image than idea, a hint of an emotional connection with a planet's past and our memories of its cherished history. The ties are not meant to be logical—just a kiss of nostalgia or a kiss of pain. And a reference to one of Byron's poems (another outside world) allows for enforcing the ambiguous conclusion, a stated and subtle reaction from those humans who have abandoned home:

> And if, at some distant, galactic gathering,
> A social event for the best of your children,

Someone casually mentions your name,
Brings back thoughts of our common home
After so many vanished forgotten years…
How will they recall you?…
Like Byron's lover,
With silence,
And tears.
　　("A Song of Distant Earth")

Summary

So, in response to our original question—can world-building occur in a poem?—the answer is a confident yes. It won't be as extensive or in as much detail, or even consistency, as in a novel. But the poetic flashes we get of it, the images whether alone or stacked, can be more instantaneous, more probing (into both the created universe itself and our own reaction to it), more like sensations that bypass the brain and dive into our secret and emotional depths, to the deeper houses of mystery whether those shadows are cosmic or not. It's a mix of planning (in the poet) and pantsing (in the reader as well as the poet), a flurry of suggestions that take us to something already built, or to something in the process of being built by the mutual participation of writer and reader. These open ties can overwhelm and make a point about new perceptions, or lead us through our creativity to, we hope, fantastic realms.

A Poem

Since most examples provided here were science-fictional, this concluding poem is a depiction of a fantasy world, in which two background cultures are suggested, one a realistic ancient setting of poor villages, and the other a near-Atlantis civilization that existed in the past—yet it's ultimately a love poem, and it even has a theme. Several of the devices covered here are demonstrated: positing a known realistic world, hinting at a larger legendary world, letting images break the confinement (especially in the backstory), and the direct appeal to emotions.

The Haunted

She stands on a barren cliff and stares
To the drowned lands far in the west,
The sunken cities and forsaken kingdoms,
Where she, daughter of an ancient race,
Once stole secrets—with her helpmate lover—
From cruel tyrants to give to the oppressed.
But, caught, she was tried and banished,
Flung to this land-gripped sullen world
Where, later, she could only watch in horror
As her Atlantean continent—and her lover—
Sank in disaster beneath the gray sea.
So that now, she stares,
Left with nothing for her endless desire.

And I, from a meager nearby village
Of poor simple folk, barely a man,
Not near enough worthy, watch her in pain,
As she, unaware of me, watches the sea.

Oh, I know she's unreachable,
Of a world not my own,
I realize my longing is naïve and selfish.
But say *not* I'm afflicted, say not that fate
Has placed her here for only the torture
Of my hopeless love.
No, I believe—I declare!—
That the *living*, and not ghosts,
Determine our obsessions.

We are not led by spirits unkind.
We *choose* our haunts.

And thus…
She is mine.

Putting the Science in Science Fiction Poetry

Jeannine Hall Gailey

I have a confession to make. Before I got my MA in English, and my MFA in Creative Writing, I had a Bachelor of Science in Biology. I got my pre-med degree in three years, taking some extra classes in things like medical botany, environmental toxicology, and other areas of interest. So yes, I was that nerd.

I started writing poems as a kid, but I was equally interested in dinosaur bones and poisonous herbs (I read my grandmother's Foxfire Books and *Farmer's Almanac* for fun.). Mentions of Cesium-137 and the cancer-causing effects of sassafras, chaos theory, fractals, and string theory started creeping into my poetry. I've always loved reading science fiction so when I discovered there was such a thing as science fiction poetry, I was elated. I joined the Science Fiction & Fantasy Poetry Association and later the Horror Writer's Association—and found so many writers who loved the same things I did, who pushed the boundaries of what *literature* was supposed to be or be about.

My favorite movies as a kid were *Star Wars: A New Hope*, *Nausicaa of the Valley of the Wind*, and *The Last Unicorn*. I read my mom's poetry and biology textbooks (she was going to school while I was little) and copies of *Bullfinch's Mythology* and *The Odyssey*, the Andrew Lang Color Fairy Book series, and books of Japanese and Chinese folk tales my father would bring back from his work travels. My father was a robotics scientist, and in our basement a Geiger counter sat on a bar and a robot arm was poised to play chess. I learned to program a TRS-80 computer when I was seven. My dad's bookshelf—unlike my mom's—wasn't lined with classics, but rather with engineering texts and "adult" science fiction—Isaac Asimov's *I Robot*, *The Time Machine*, as well as Ray Bradbury's *Illustrated Man* and *Fahrenheit 451*.

As I started to learn to write poetry, I accumulated books by Emily Dickinson, Edna St. Vincent Millay, Carl Sandburg—but I never forgot my earliest loves of science fiction, mythology, and fairy tales, so my first poems had cats who talked to space ships, time-traveling unicorns, and characters who couldn't escape from fairy-tale tropes. This was when I was still in grade school, and no one had told me yet that this was the "wrong" subject matter for poetry.

When I studied poetry in college, I discovered new-to-me writers—Margaret Atwood, Louise Gluck, Lucille Clifton, Sylvia Plath—who used mythology and even superhero characters in *personas*—which would be a key for me to figure out how to tell my own story—through the voices of superheroes and supervillains, folk tale characters, mythological figures.

One of my MA program professors, after I turned in an early version of a poem about my father's work with robots and radiation, which would later become "Chaos Theory," told me that scientific language was *difficult* to put into poetry "because the heavy, clunky Latinate words, were hard to scan." He meant they were hard to fit into certain forms, but I took this as a challenge and never stopped using "clunky Latinate" science vocabulary in my work. Here's a piece of the poem we discussed, from "Chaos Theory," a poem in my first book, *Becoming the Villainess*:

"…Ordering chaos was my father's talisman;
He told us about the garden of the janitor
at the Fernald Superfund site, where mutations
burgeoned in the soil like fractal branchings.

The dahlias and tomatoes he showed to my father,
doubling and tripling in size and variety,
magentas, pinks and reds so bright they blinded,

churning offspring gigantic and marvelous
from that ground sick with uranium.
The janitor smiled proudly. My father nodded…In his mind he watched
the man's DNA

unraveling, patching itself together again
with wobbling sentry enzymes…"

Though this poem stays firmly in the scientific world, it asks readers to imagine things unseen, putting it in the realm of speculative writing.

As far as addressing my former professor's distaste for using scientific language in poetry, I am far from alone—Tracy K. Smith's *Life on Mars*, which won the 2012 Pulitzer Prize for Poetry, makes liberal use of this kind of language, as do many of my contemporaries. Poetry is big enough to contain multitudes—and this includes all kinds of vocabularies, scientific and medical included.

When I teach, I often encourage people to embrace subject matters and vocabularies they've been told are off limits. My first book, *Becoming the Villainess*, contained poems about comic book characters and cosmic mutations, while my latest book, *Field Guide to the End of the World,* was all about surviving various kinds of apocalypses—there were plagues, nuclear winter, war, famine, meteors, aliens…But probably the book I'd say most heavily relies on science and scientific language is *The Robot Scientist's Daughter*. The following two poems from that book will be used as examples of my scientific speculative poetry.

This next poem might be considered strictly scientific, rather than science fiction. I felt like it captured the lyric impulse, even with that so-called *bulky* scientific language. I'm including an excerpt of the poem, the second stanza of "Cesium Burns Blue:"

In my back yard, they lit cesium
to measure the glow.
Hold it in your hand:
foxfire, wormwood, glow worm.
Cesium lights the rain,
absorbed in the skin,
unstable, unstable
dancing away, ticking away
in bones, fingernails, brain.
Sick burns through, burns blue.

Once again, this poem uses true scientific facts, but asks the reader to imagine beyond the facts, asking them to "speculate" about what happens to an animal when it is exposed to a radioactive toxin.

In *The Robot Scientist's Daughter*, I concocted an imaginary persona for the book—and put her in a variety of situations. In the next poem, when she gets sick of her malfunctioning human body, she builds herself a new mechanical body, and transforms herself.

The Robot Scientist's Daughter [medical wonder]

was a bit confused. She started down a road
to medical wonder, sat under the machine's lights,
but then tiptoed off on a paper trail,
looking for an island of cranes. She made a thousand
wishes, still she shed a blue glow
and everyone said *how sickly*. Her nails
made of plastic and paper maché, her heart's
thump-thump three times fast. Her one kidney
curled inside her ribs, her blood trying to escape.
"Father" she screamed but he couldn't save her.

The robot scientist's daughter knew
what she had to do. With her own two hands
she built a new body, one that worked better
this time, silver and shiny and smooth
as mirrored glass. After all she'd been trained,
it was no less than was expected. She crawled inside
and adjusted the fit. This time, there will be no
stopping her. The curves are all impenetrable
and the precision of each drum-kit-beat keeps her in line.
She's a soldier, a savior, a ship to bear prisoners into space.

This poem takes the leap from science-to-science fiction; the Robot Scientist's Daughter character, knowing her body is corrupted by health problems, uses her knowledge of robotics to build a new mecha self. In the poem, I refer to real-life medical problems, but include more fantastic elements in order to move it from autobiography to speculative verse. The tone of the poem changes, too.

This last poem, from my most recent book, *Field Guide to the End of the World*, jumps into a speculative future dystopia, where the imaginary title character writes to a (possibly dead) love interest.

The Last Love Poem

I am obsolete as my ancestors, the Appalachian glass blowers,
provoking fire over and over to produce their artifacts.

76

I knew no writing could survive when we started calling children "vectors,"
when our own forests grew heavy with toxic spores.
A map? A list? A series of images? What could I write now
that would do anything? A poem orphaned, a crystalline ornament

with no Christmas in sight, swirled with delicate color, resting
gently on a ledge until the inevitable smash…
So here in my last moments, let me set down my memories of you:
your rough skin, your green eyes, your slightly clumsy hands.
We turned and smiled at each other on the ugly concrete glinting with broken glass
as someone yelled obscenities and someone else handed out pizza slices to strangers.
When we ran out of flour, we learned to bake cookies out of nuts, seeds, flowers.
We decided, against all odds, to plant dahlias.
Do you see this as a rebellion? That after all this, the poet clings, stubborn,
to romance, to the idea that somehow a small connection,

a tiny universe of fire and friction, might be preserved?

This poem from *Field Guide to the End of the World* is firmly in the science fiction category, as it includes an imaginary apocalyptic future. But would you call it a scientific poem? There are references to vectors and to toxic spores but no specific element names or medical conditions. What do you think?

I happen to have a primary immune deficiency and multiple sclerosis, which meant that, more than most people, I was going to have to stay in during the pandemic. The last book of poetry I published, *Field Guide to the End of the World*, was a tongue-in-cheek guide to surviving apocalypses; now that I was in the middle of one, what was there to write? Why, explore pandemics, of course! From a spiritual angle, a political angle, a scientific angle…that's the book I'm working on now. Since I actually have had an active interest in virology since I was a college student, I'm still reading articles about coronavirus variants and immune-challenged-people's responses to vaccines and that sort of thing almost every day. I'm sure I'm not the only person who will have the scientific language of pandemics leaching into their work in the near future.

I hope that through a growing awareness of how science and science fiction impact our daily lives—from climate change dystopias to pandemic apocalypses—that we will see more poetry that crosses over the mainstream, to include a poetry with scientific and science fiction vocabularies and awareness.

Like Fright on Lice:
Humor and Horror Poetry

Michael Arnzen

Turn the Urn

Do you know what doggerel is?

It's dogshit poetry.

At least that's my mnemonic. But doggerel is the first thing that comes to mind when I think of "humorous" poetry and no matter how demonic your horror writing might be—no matter how devious or demented—you probably don't want to be accused of producing crap. Most definitions of doggerel suggest that it not only refers to goofy poetry, but also to poetry *so bad it's funny*. The Poetry Foundation says it is "bad verse traditionally characterized by clichés, clumsiness and irregular meter" and—because of those three things—is "unintentionally" humorous. The writer becomes the butt of his own jokes. *Merriam-Webster* just bluntly calls it "trivial" or "inferior" poetry. Because good poetry is supposed to be the serious, gorgeous stuff that only a master of language could produce, and not something funny, intentionally or not.

There's an "aesthetic" to traditional poetry—an assumption that writing a poem is a kind of game, controlled by certain lyrical forms or rules, which are difficult to master. But in that form lurks the very essence of beauty, and that's why horror poetry—especially humorous horror poetry—gets a bad rap as doggerel.

There are plenty of poets working in the genre who actually have written eloquent, lyrical poetry that should by all rights be studied by the literati. But even poets like Clark Ashton Smith or Charles Baudelaire produce "doggerel" according to literary nerds, because these dark fantasy writers dared to fantasize, to treat imaginary creatures as real and take them in earnest. Whimsical thinking has often been aligned with foolishness. The literary school of Poststructuralism dismantled the religiously stiff following of "rules" among the poetic literati, but a suspicion of fantasy remains: the appreciation of forms

78

and "serious" (realistic) subjects continues to dominate the very idea of what a poem should be. Even in the realms of today's "free verse" poetry, these conceits (seriousness, realism) give poetry gravitas in a culture that, frankly, doesn't read a lot of poetry outside of fluffy Hallmark cards.

I say all this as a precursor to saying screw them, and write whatever you want, but if you are just getting started you should know what you are about to step into. It might leave a stink on you.

Obviously, we horror poets know that writing verse is not simply the art of eloquently waxing in rhyming phrases about beauty, nature, love and all that heady, angsty stuff you might have seen in the *Norton Anthology of British Literature.* Horror is and always has been about showing the "other side" (the dark side, the masked side, the backside) of reality. We are the outlaw bikers at the literary tea party. The people who think all funny poetry is bad poetry are those who think all poetry is rule-based, controlled by form, and concerned with beauty, wrought into fanciful shape like the ornate etchings detailed around Keats' infamous "Grecian Urn." The images on that urn tell a story as Keats spins the urn around. But we horror writers, well, we are more concerned with what is INSIDE the urn than with the fancy pictures plastered on the outside of it. And most of us are willing to smash that urn right on the ground to see what shape the ashes might take.

But I don't mean to mock literary poetry too much, because all poetry should be a literary playground for a writer, and horror writers shouldn't be excluded from playing there. Our playground just happens to be atop graveyard soil. We toy with horror's many fine and frightful tropes, bringing our gallows humor to the table. The methods of humorous horror poetry are as diverse as its many voices, so it's difficult to really teach in an article like this one. But it is the "worldview" of the horror writer, as much as the genre's many conventions, that hold us all together, no matter how literary or silly we might strive to be. We're all gazing into the same abyss. Some of us see terrifying monsters and need to warn others about them. Others peer into the abyss and cackle with insane glee at how marvelous the strange can be, and even, perhaps, how beautiful.

So the first lesson for all horror poets is not just to avoid doggerel but to actually closely study the way poets give shape to fear. The best way to do that is to read this whole book first, then read lots of published poetry collections (and I mean everything from the classic graveyard poets of the 1800s to the indie fantasy poets working today), and then practice, practice, practice. Figure out what makes sonnets tick, and how to pronounce the word "pantoum." Know the rules. Play the role of a literary writer, even though you're wearing a witch's hat and a warlock's robe at night. Know the rules and cast them like spells. Then play with abandon and break those rules all you want. The confidence, the muscle memory, the knowledge—it'll all be there, supporting your lines, even if you're writing the equivalent of a body horror fart joke.

Horror poets who want to write funny stuff should read lots of funny stuff, just to develop a sense of what it feels like and an understanding of what makes it tick. Of course, there is a long tradition of humorous verse, much of which appears in children's literature. Just think of the bizarro words in any Dr. Seuss story and you'll know what I'm talking about. The "poetry" of Dr. Seuss is comedic because it uses rhyme in unexpected ways to capture a fantastic world of the author's creation. A lot of it is merely suggestion, rather than direct depiction (in what universe are eggs and ham *green*? In what world do cats *wear hats* and where are they off to in them?), but what's key to Seussian humor is that the absurd is taken for granted as a kind of normalcy, a reality with its own rules that are a wonder to behold. And of course, what makes the absurdity funny (and not just fantastical) in the first place is that that reality is filled with what are called "category mistakes." Green ham is rotten ham in the "real" world, but normal in Sam-I-Am's. And of course, even the rules of language are violated— I am Sam is rendered Sam I Am, in an inversion of order. It's clever and witty wordplay, gleefully celebrating the quirks of language. It's not entirely scary, but it could be if taken seriously. (Indeed, Seuss could be devilish and bizarro in his own right—look for his musical, *The 5,000 Fingers of Dr. T*).

Seuss is just the bloody tip of a sharp iceberg. Read. A lot. Everyone tells you this, and it's the sagest wisdom in the world for a writer. Just as a musician needs to listen to lots of music to tune their ear for their instrument, so too must writers read, from the canonical to the contemporary. But if you're writing humorous horror you need to hunt down the funny stuff. This need not be limited to comedic poetry, though you'll want to read that, too. No, but funny horror— and dark humor—is definitely something to savor on your poetry writing tongue and let it melt into your mind. You could root around among YA and Children's literature for some fun dark fiction (Roald Dahl or Edward Gorey are good ones to start with). Search the categories of humor and comedy and see what turns up for inspiration. Anything riffing on the title "Die Laughing" or making puns on death, disease, and disturbance is probably going to be in the right vein. Read the hilarious horror fiction of Jeff Strand, Martin Mull, Grady Hendrix, Mona Awad, Kelly Devos—and wacky bizarro work by D. Harlan Wilson, Carlton Mellick

III, Kevin Donihe, and beyond. Dig around and *read who they read*. And in all your research, be sure to tune in to any *poets* you stumble upon in magazines and anthologies who make you chuckle darkly; buy their books.

There's actually a lot of horror comedy in visual media. Everything from goofy movies like *Abbott and Costello Meet Frankenstein* to the *Addams Family* TV show to Mel Brooks' *Young Frankenstein* are game for fueling your creative furnace, so don't overlook them. Let these things steep in your brain like sugary tea. If it's too much juvenilia, worry not: you can still bring the adult perspective to your own creations, while also indulging the inner child who likes to laugh.

Again, not everything needs to be horror-adjacent either; sometimes you can find inspiration in the downright goofy. I mean, they remade the children's show, *The Banana Splits*, into a serious splatter film recently—so anything goes, right? Anthologies of humor, whether in the horror genre or not, are sure to give you a wide array of fruitful examples. I think the best of this kind is *Seriously Funny* (edited by Barbara Hamby and David Kirby), which includes a number of today's best poets riffing on love, life, death and everything in between. Or even try memoirs with a dark jester at the keyboard, like *Furiously Happy* by Jenny Lawson, or virtually anything penned (or better yet, recorded to audio) by your favorite stand-up comedian or skit performer (for me, it's George Carlin, whose album *You're All Diseased* might as well be a title on the horror shelf).

But some of these aren't poets, you might retort, *and a lot of this isn't horror!* It doesn't matter (so long as you're actually reading horror fiction, too). To write good humor, you have to immerse yourself in the work of other humorists and come out dripping with an ironic, sarcastic, sardonic mindset all your own. Humor is a worldview, a perspective, that we bring to our dark poetry. And when you do this, you might actually have something new to say; you might be the next George Carlin of horror! Cultivate that hilarious worldview however you can. Don't just read humor. Watch bad comedies on Netflix, habitually tune in to *SNL* every weekend, and surf YouTube for "Funny-or-Die" clips and scroll TikTok for more. Go where the laughter is, gorge on your studies...and then spit those feelings back up at the keyboard. Laughter, like your sickness, is contagious!

Or better yet: you're like a witch casting a very peculiar kind of spell when you write horror poetry. It takes practice, but it will come more naturally if you can persistently conjure irreverence and cackle with glee.

Some Peculiar Tips

Okay, having said all that, there are some tendencies, and some tricks to the trade you can try, that often can produce hilarious results. But remember: there is no formula for humor. You just have to come at a topic from a bent angle and have a willingness to pursue the logic of things to their extreme and absurd ends, not to mention laugh at that which others might take seriously, including the hardest thing of all—yourself.

Indeed, the comedy of horror poetry is often centered in a *peculiar perspective*. Imagine a poem talking about a man transforming into a werewolf. You could have a lot of fun describing bones buckling, claws extending, and bloodlust percolating. That's the joy of writing horror poetry: describing the pain, the gore, the body *in extremis*, while appealing to the reader's senses, making them feel things they might not ever feel, feeding into their morbid curiosity. Comedy takes it one step further. What peculiar perspective can you bring to the scenario just described?

Well, think of all the variables for point of view. There's the man, transforming under moonlight. And then there's the wolf he's becoming. Depicting how he perceives these changes would be fantastic, and potentially funny, as he processes the strangeness of his situation even as he's suffering through it. Mostly because he'd probably feel detached from his own body. But this is a conventional viewpoint in dark fantasy, not a peculiar one *per se*. You could make him a peculiar person, put in *an ironic position*. So what if he were a barber, ironically growing an absurd amount of hair everywhere? Maybe he'd become obsessed with cutting it, even as it was growing from him. Picture that. Silly, and impossible and horrifying.

Or what if your peculiar perspective were something else in the room? Like, say, his wife, jaded by the whole thing, which she's seen a hundred times before? Then you'd have the *comedy of incongruity*—or, more specifically here, *an opposing sentiment*—the opposite expression of what one would normally expect in this context—a woman not horrified or frightened, but strangely bored by the routine of it all. Oppositions like these are the stuff of *sarcasm and bemused detachment*, which is inherently funny as well. Or what if the poem were told from another "person" who frequently sees men transform into wolves? What if it were told from the viewpoint of the moon itself? That might be funniest of all, as it is truly absurd, and yet it's also the most detached observer of them all. Choose a peculiar perspective character or narrator and give them a realistic voice, perhaps one entirely "inappropriate" for the situation being depicted, and you're spinning comedy gold.

Not all poetry is so character-centered though, and sometimes the peculiar perspective is simply the unseen narrator's (ostensibly the poet's, or the persona they're adopting, anyway), writing "objectively" from a distance. In this case, description and prose style becomes everything, and beyond the dark jesting of the narrator, the language itself must be funny. There are words that are funny words. Sometimes these words just sound funny (i.e., there's some "attitude" they carry that is goofy, inappropriate for the context, or is simply a weird choice given the moment of the line). The way some words call attention to themselves can make the poem feel like the writer is just performing "word play" rather than treating the theme seriously, and while it can often backfire, sometimes puns can make a horror poem deliver a chill.

Take, for instance, my poem, "Fuzzy Bunnies." I wrote this in response to my grandmother, poor sweet woman, who once read my work and said, "You're such a good writer, Michael, but...why can't you just write about warm, fuzzy bunnies?" I laughed and said no, but then I tried it later that night, and the result was this poem, which people often tell me is their favorite of mine:

Fuzzy Bunnies

The eyes roll back
and accusingly glare
when my feet slide forward
and hot rabbit innards
squirt between my toes
only then do I see
why these furry white skins
are called slippers

(I remember a teacher telling me that she read this poem to her class on Easter, and I found that hilarious.)

I don't know how "funny" such an extremely disgusting poem is, but it certainly falls in the category of humorous horror, for several reasons. Some words I'd identify as "funny words" in this poem are "innards" and "squirt"—words that sound like dirty words; words that make you snarl or do wet slippery things with your mouth when you say them out loud. Horror does that a lot: it revels in things that make you *literally* go "ewwwww" by referring to visceral acts by using words that, when you read them out loud, perform something that calls attention to the body. There's a music to the musing of poetry and humor plays some offbeat "notes." Sometimes it will invert the feelings in a way that makes us feel like something funny is going on with the writing. Sometimes, too, a funny poem will use tongue twisters that make us laugh at the repetition and the way a reader might trip up.

But on top of all that is the final pun: the "twist ending" of "Fuzzy Bunnies" is that last line where the word "slippers" is taken literally in a way that drives home the disgusting act that has just been described. And this is exactly the stuff of humorous horror: when the figurative is treated as if it were real (and vice versa). Yes, "slippers" refer to slipping a soft shoe onto our bare feet, but what if slippers were slippery? And why would they be that way? The sickest, most extreme answer I could come up with was "because they're bunny slippers...and not just fur, but freshly killed rabbit."

The comedy here is delivered not merely through funny words, but also over-the-top description. It is *excessive*. Humorous horror poems will not just describe a moment of gore, they will revel in it, going *over-the-top*—beyond the amount needed to deliver the message. It is almost like a fetish, an indulgence of the morbid. In the bunny poem, "the eyes roll up" in a literal eyeroll as if the dead animal were still alive, saying *Come on! Really?!* from beyond the grave.

This kind of excess and indulgence often reveals the presence of what Edgar Allan Poe called "*the imp of the perverse*" at play. I assume you noticed the peculiar perspective of the narrator. That's the perverse imp! And it is a disturbing position for the reader to occupy, as you indulge their *taboo desire* (or morbid curiosity to know what it might feel like to step into a dead animal) for just a small moment of time. While the narrator engages in diabolical glee, the reader might laugh nervously or say "ewww, that's sick" and titter with glee like a child who laughs at a dead baby joke.

Horror and humorous wordplay go together like fright on lice, and poetry is the format that best puts a spotlight on language.

But beyond funny words and twisted puns, beyond excessive description and inappropriate indulgences, horror can also adopt a humorous mode when it engages in parody or mockery of a familiar person, place, or thing. And sometimes humorous horror can take the absurd seriously, or vice-versa, to good effect. Consider this poem, for instance:

Michael Arnzen

The Fall Down the Stairs of The House of Usher

When I push her down the stairs
she swims in the air for a moment
like we're dancing
and I play a little song in my head
to accompany it
before the erratic thud of her skull
against the steps
breaks my waltzing daydream
with its own offbeat tempo
and I hear another voice sing
as I stumble forward

This poem is relatively serious and, I hope, creepy, but the title makes fun of Poe's classic story, "The Fall of the House of Usher," by a) making it even longer than it is and really ever ought to be, thereby mocking Poe's long-windedness, and b) trivializing the somber tone and hint of the fantastic with the everyday act of falling down some stairs. I've made the fantasy more familiar, more domestic. This is a common method of horror comedy. Tripping down stairs (or simply falling from heights, or any injury, really) is also a universal fear; indeed, it is one far more "realistic" than the "fantastic" house of Usher, with its ghostly implications. When I invented this, I came up with the title first as a kind of *parody*. But then I took the absurd and goofy title seriously (and this *inappropriate mood for the context* is often what makes things funny: being serious when one should be laid back or being frivolous when one should be serious and sober). One must honor their literary forefathers, I think, even if they intend to tear them a new one. So, thanks to my respect for the aura of Poe, the parody became more of a loving homage, even if it remained an Arnzen poem through and through, and the horror of it all came to me as I wrote the final lines where the presence of a sinister spectre is implied after all. In fact, I often discover the horror while I'm writing—it's like my unconscious mind is compelled to "go there." (My friends always try to shame me by saying, "Oh Arnzen, *you had to go there*" when I say something dark and inappropriate...but my answer is always, "Yes, that's what I do for a living.")

Believe it or not, there's a detailed literary analysis of my "Fall Down the Stairs" poem you can find in the back pages of the hardcover edition of my collection, *The Gorelets Omnibus*, written by Rich Ristow. So read that if you want to glean more lessons about what makes that poem tick as a work of horror poetry. I bring Ristow's analysis up here, however, because he makes the point that my tendency toward imagery borrows heavily from the approach of William Carlos Williams as much as Poe, whose minimalism is evident in his classic poem, "The Red Wheelbarrow." Look for that online, if you aren't already familiar with it (be sure to also call up his far more sinister ditty, "This is Just To Say"—or if you're looking for something weird, seek his funeral poem, "Tract"). Anyway, I have to admit: I felt "seen" by Ristow. I was outed as a minimalist, who had learned from Williams. I like to employ the tactics of the Imagist school of poetry in the realm of horror, letting images that one ought not to normally spend time with (such as gashes in the belly, monstrous tentacles, or decapitated heads) dominate the poem and speak for themselves, while also keeping the language relatively simple and succinct. And more importantly, this approach can suggest a context that isn't obvious in the poem, but which the reader must imagine for themselves with dawning terror or dread. In a way this is a *parody* of the approach of a literary poet (in this case, Williams), and I think that's always a valid way of drumming up new ideas, new shapes, and also hilarious results. Here's one I posted to twitter just this week:

son, put on your hat,
and oh,
one last thing:

don't eat
the bloody snow
either

You can see in this untitled poem the sly allusion to William's frequent stanza shape and the way he depicts a mundane situation (such as putting a hat on the head of a child heading out to the snow) that in the end takes a "turn" toward an *implied* meaning that transcends the mundane (in this case, the unexpected reference to *bloody* snow).

But it's also just a silly rewrite of the already somewhat funny expression, "Don't eat the yellow snow" (which might explain the "either" at the end of it). It's funny because it's scatological. While "going for the gross-out" can be read as too easy, too juvenile, too "beneath" you, in comedy we get more animalistic than most other forms. So referencing the dirty and secret parts of our bodies "down there" is common—horror writers don't only "have to go there," they also have to go "down" there. We delve into things that should not be discussed in "polite" society. Referencing the taboo—perhaps subtly, perhaps just momentarily—makes readers a little uncomfortable and they might respond with tittering and giggles just because of that.

So in this poem, blood makes it even worse, not just because it's a reference to bodily fluids, but because the loss of such fluids suggests death in a way that yellow snow does not—though in both there's a hint of bad hygiene, obviously—and contagion. And if you find yourself asking what makes the snow bloody, and why is the narrator so calmly mentioning it while telling his child to avoid it, then you're reading it correctly. There is no answer. Perhaps the speaker has committed a murder (maybe by running someone over with a wheelbarrow?) and is saying "pay no heed" to the evidence. Or maybe this is a vampire world, and the child is a hungry young Vlad. I'm not telling. It's funny to imagine the absurd explanations for this absurd situation. Exploiting the reader's sense of wonder about the unknowable and encouraging them to think the worst is what we do.

In my mind, that simple little poem hits the right balance between humor and horror, and balance is something I recommend you aim for, particularly at the end of a piece: because it leaves the reader uncertain whether to laugh or scream, to double over or to back away, double-time. The uncertainty is dark, leaving the reader guessing, and I think that's as satisfying at the end of a poem as a great "twist ending." And it often has the happy side-effect of sending the reader right back to the top of the poem, seeking answers, and appreciating the craft of the poem along the way, perhaps even catching subtle jokes, double-meanings, double entendres, and more.

Some Pitiful Pitfalls:
Don't succumb to silliness.
Humorous horror poetry can be a dangerous game. While there's no Poetry Police to punish you for making innocent blunders, readers are pretty unforgiving, and if you tell a bad or offensive joke in a poem, they are likely to avoid your byline afterward. It's probably wise to avoid being goofy for goof's sake and marketing the equivalent of juvenile verse (even if the themes are Rated-R) to adult markets.

And while I would never say there are any hard or fast rules that can't be broken, it's generally true that there are poetic forms like the limerick or the nursery rhyme that just don't work very well in horror poetry. It depends on the context, of course ("There once was a man from Providence..." Possibly okay for a Lovecraft fanzine, but likely not appropriate for a mainstream or more serious poetry market like the journal *Dreams and Nightmares* or *Uncanny Magazine*). And there are limited audiences for more experimental approaches like concrete poems (poems that are laid out on the page like an image, say, an arrangement of lettering into a sea-shell-like spiral) or neologistic poems—that is, poetry consisting of made-up words like those we find in the classic Lewis Carroll poem, "Jabberwocky." Such approaches might be funny, but usually aren't familiar enough to horror readers. And that's the catch with genre poetry: you are writing for an audience of fiction readers and film fans—general genre consumers—so play in their ball field and you'll be okay. But don't succumb to the sillier side of poetry if you can avoid it.

Avoid the Inside Joke

Horror poetry is indeed poetry for genre fans; it borrows tropes and familiar icons from the narrative universe of horror fiction and the cinematic world of horror cinema and, well, plays within it, poetically. It is inherently part of the job to reference genre conventions but be careful not to be so referential that only the most devout of fans will "get" what you're doing. This is not a puzzle for an elite tribe. It is a vehicle for a message, even if that message is an ironic jab or mocking punch at something. Don't make it a clown car crowded with sly allusions to another horror text that only a scholar at Brown University would be able to uncover in their research. It's hard to be funny if the reader literally won't "get" the reference. The problem with inside jokes is that they don't just require a certain kind of previous knowledge that your reader might not have, but they are also inherently exclusionary and self-congratulatory. The sort of joke that only an elite group might get. Don't write that flap trap. People read to connect with other people, and the last thing you want to do is write only for a few who "get you." The root of the word "publishing" is "public." Invite all readers into the circus tent to share in your wit and entertain them.

There are a few exceptions, of course. One or two insider references often are fine, just as it is okay to use big words (i.e., specialized terminology) once in a while. But just as you might surround nomenclature (let's say, a term for some medical instrument) with enough context to keep the meaning clear, you should do the same for your deep reference. Heck, maybe your reader will be motivated to research the topic further. But how many times have you done that with something a poet mentioned? Rarely, I'd wager. Poems need to be brief and self-contained.

Another exception to the "inside joke" rule is when you are specifically writing for a limited market, where it is almost guaranteed that the reader will get your allusions to other texts. If you're crafting a poem for a Lovecraft-inspired anthology, or penning a piece for a vampire magazine, you can probably get away with your funny stanza that rhymes "hearsecloth" with Azathoth, or a poem formatted like a recipe that makes some joke about substitutes for garlic when preparing a baby for a midnight snack.

Avoid Punching Down

Just as inside jokes might exclude many readers, pushing them away from the genre instead of inviting them to laugh alongside you, sometimes humorists "punch down" without realizing it, and often they are encouraged to "punch up" instead.

What's with all this punching, Rocky?

Well, you've heard of the phrase "punch line," right? That's the zinger at the end of the joke; the unexpected bit that the audience (hopefully) doesn't see coming. It's the equivalent of a "twist ending" in a horror story—and in horror fiction the punch line is often one rife with dreadful import, or gory surprise, and we might as well call it a "slash line."

But the phrases "punch up" and "punch down" are what comedians say when they are talking about the butt of the joke. Are you making fun of the king, the president, anyone in power who might actually be oppressing us? If so, then you're punching up, and on behalf of the common folk, let me thank you. But if you "punch down" you assume the air of superiority and might come across as a bully, by, say, mocking the handicapped, or telling jokes that are essentially racist, sexist, agist or any of the other -ists that signify targeting a group that is not dominant or in power. Humorists can get in trouble when they play politics, and yes, everyone is fair game who takes themselves too seriously.... a lot of great horror literature is social *satire*. But be careful and think about who you might be insulting among your audience when you go for the punch. Do they deserve it?

Don't Drone On

Ever listen to a comedian tell a really long joke? It usually consists of many short jokes, signaled by pauses for laughter. Think about the way stand-ups structure their monologues and emulate the timing, perhaps using stanzas and line breaks to pace the humorous delivery as appropriate. Timing, as they say, is the secret to comedy. But I'd say it's not so much the pace of the poem but the length of it that matters most. A poem too lengthy tests the reader's patience and often kills a good joke. The brevity of the moment matters. Keep things tight and short.

Like a good noose.

Around the neck of your doggerel.

The Shape of Horror Fiction as a Knock-Knock Joke

Knock Knock
Who's There?
<silence>
Knock Knock
Who's There?
<silence>
Knock Knock
For Christ's Sake! <you open the door>
<dismembered hand flies up and chokes you>

Instigation Prompts:

- Write a poem that uses the ludicrous phrase "Appease the Tentacle" as either a title or a final line.
- Mock a horror trope of your choice by taunting it in a sing-songy children's rhyme of your own design.
- Murder a clown, hilariously.
- Write a suicide note by someone who is having trouble settling on a method.
- Write a parody of song lyrics, by substituting horror concepts for the familiar lines.

Dark Poetry and War

Alessandro Manzetti

Poetry has always told of war, from Homer's *Iliad* and its focus on the Trojan War, to the verses by Walt Whitman and Emily Dickinson (and also Melville) on the American Civil War, to the many great authors who portrayed the First and Second World Wars (Apollinaire, Brecht, Sassoon, Rilke, Hardy, Eliot, Yeats, and the Italians Quasimodo and Ungaretti), and poets have presented us with many varying interpretations of war, among them testimonial poems and verses of remembrance, memories, and of opposition. Themes such as dictatorial regimes and modern civil wars (Neruda) lead up to the Beat Generation (Ginsberg, Corso) with its invectives against the Vietnam War. Contemporary poetry abounds on the Arab-Israeli conflicts (Mahmoud Darwish), the war in Iraq and other Middle Eastern countries (Nizar Qabbani, Dunya Mikhail), and on other highly topical issues. Specific war events have also formed their own literary schools, such as the Japanese Genbaku Bungaku (Tōge Sankichi, Shoda Shinoe and Kurihara Sadako), based on the experience of atomic bombs, and those which reflect on the Holocaust (Paul Celan, Elie Wiesel, Geoffrey Hill and Primo Levi).

Writing and/or incorporating war/action into speculative dark poetry is a tough challenge, as it touches on themes of great relevance and sensitivity. Rendering the action on the page, like in fiction, is particularly difficult here as it requires the writer to employ great visual and cinematic ability. I have dealt with this challenge several times, both in fiction and in poetry. For the latter, I penned a collection dedicated to the theme of war (entitled *WAR*), co-written with poet Marge Simon. In it we attempted to guide the reader on a journey through different conflicts across the eras, from the times of the conquistadors to the various civil wars, WW1 and WW2, Vietnam, the war in Iraq, up to contemporary Middle Eastern conflicts.

This journey, which also details some specific events and battles (Stalingrad, Vukovar), is characterized by its focus on small settings, thereby deepening the vividness of each detail presented—as if we had a camera on our shoulders, capturing individual frames to portray the deepest and widest possible range of emotion within the characters. We didn't define this only by action, simply throwing the reader onto the battlefield. Instead we tried to depict the experiences of individuals who found themselves in a wider range of 'war' scenarios than just those more typically known. I'm talking about traumas, the changing world around us, and about loss—both of personal identity, and of loved ones. I'm also talking about cynicism, brutality, and the horrors of the human dark side, and all the consequences that follow once it is unleashed. I believe this is one of the keys to contemporary interpretation of this difficult theme: the specificity of these more intimate experiences. Readers already have their 'global' image of war, something like a bird's-eye view of wars and their related events, formed by school education and further detailed with the written and visual supplementary information available today to all, especially where modern and contemporary events are concerned. The poet's role therefore is not to offer the same kind of material, peppered only with personal and political considerations, but instead to hone in on the single bombed house, enter it through a window, and capture the various humanities extant within—presenting these details to the reader as they are, allowing readers to witness and live these realities, crystallized by time, as if they were themselves in that same place, at the same moment.

But now let's explore the details and complexities of these forms of poetic composition, starting with the theme of War, to uncover useful keys that may open doors to new interpretations. From there we'll move towards another element this article aims to highlight: the management of action, and the various possible ways by which the action meets and blends with the theme itself.

First of all, it is essential to keep in mind that the poet's own era is an integral part of who he is himself. We are each recorders of our own emotions, we are contemporary human beings, and so in terms of language, the poets' work must be closely connected to his own time to be truly heard. Even if we are writing verses about the well-known conquistador Hernán Cortés, perhaps to portray his escape from Tenochtitlán with his men and horses loaded with gold, or about Achilles dragging Hector's corpse around the walls of Troy, we are always children of our time, and this should never be forgotten. A poet is able to portray events and moods of distant eras, but the traveler we seat in our time machine is a contemporary, as are his ears, brain, education, and reading experiences. The courtly form—the one that often defines the imagination of the reader not accustomed to modern and contemporary poetry—has nothing to do with the contemporary world, with the voices of the street and the terms we use in everyday life. Minimalism is the true secret of poetry: that is, summarizing and encapsulating entire worlds or ranges of emotion in one line, or in two words, whilst taking care of the rhythm, tempo, and lyrical tone of the myriad possible combinations. The contemporary dark poet, a son of his own time and of a twentieth century that has already shown so much in poetry and literature (to him as well as to the readers themselves), can only forge verses free of obsolete forms and pre-established styles, which repel readers of poetry, be they firm enthusiasts or those approaching poetry for the first time. Poetry has always been avant-garde, as a form of communication and literature. It inspires fiction itself to break new boundaries. Minimalism and the topicality of themes are primary keys to the whole process of poetic creation.

Going back to the theme of war as it applies to a poetic work, once the main theme has been chosen, it is then necessary to define the possible depths down which the reader might be lead. The siege of Stalingrad, for example, immediately recalls images of snow and hunger, the German panzers, the explosions, the Red Army snipers. All of this is known and is easily accessible through documentaries and historical records. For the poet to offer a different contribution, he will have to turn his pen into a sort of telescopic lens, showing the detail of the bruised faces, the frozen hands, those last in line waiting to receive a meager ration. He must invite the reader to enter a room and identify smells and sounds; dissect the characters (and the settings); offer a piece of history that the reader can share. Using the idea of cameras and how they may frame a scene, a character, a puddle, a fly, can be useful for the poet as this helps him avoid limiting his lines to a blank, predictable description that leaves the reader sitting comfortably in an armchair as he reads our book. Let's instead guide him through the streets of a city, between the barricades, involving him with the stories and sequences of little things, of people, casting our lens across the lights and the shadows. Everything else around a war—the soldiers, the dead—must be perceived as a background symphony. We write about microscopic, personal things. We are not writing war reports. Human emotions (like memories) are evoked by smells, music, colors, and details, not by battle scenes or macroscopic realities, and this is true in everyday life for each of us. The poet must use these small and powerful tools when embedding them in a war scenario. The dark mood applied to a poetry composition is characterized by the choice of what our 'cameras' are framing.

The dark side, death, loss, pain, blood, hunger, madness, corpses, the unknown, forced cannibalism (as in the example of Stalingrad), the personification of strong emotions in imaginary creatures or delusions of the mind—they are obviously 'dark' ingredients that must be combined, alternating with scenes of raw realism in a dark duet where one element strengthens the other, increasing the tension. Dark elements must be maintained throughout; the final lines of a composition must summarize that kind of nature without disconnecting from it to become merely moral or by giving too many explanations. The shadow must lurk—the reader must feel its darkness and malevolence, and give himself his answers, and these answers will always be different. No judgment: the facts must speak both for the victims and the killers, the prey and the predators, who sometimes—especially in war—are known to switch sides. All of this must be done without widening the scope too much on the target of our imaginary camera: be it a man, a woman, a child, an officer, a sniper, whichever existence we have chosen to frame beneath our magnifying glass among the explosions or the shouts of marching soldiers. What we offer are extracts taken from something bigger, the things that are often passed over in silence in other forms of communication. The poet sees and shares these hidden things, moving between the folds of reality, leaning out from behind the dark corner to tell what happened down that long-forgotten alley.

As for capturing an action scene in a poem, this is best done cinematically. In motion and in stills, in a mixture of the two, the poet must alternate between the poetic stanzas that frame the dynamism of the action and the absence of any movement when the action has ended or is about to begin. All meaningful frames must be presented, selecting our 'splinters' of action or inaction without slavishly following a determined and continuous timeline documenting every single moment, as this is a way more suitable for another type of fiction. We're talking about poetry, which is a different kind of animal. As an example, I recommend thinking about another form of art—painting. Specifically, impressionism. The impressionist painter (who has much in common with the poet) doesn't portray a person, a building, or a ship in a photographic way, outlining all the details with the utmost realism. He would be able to do that if he chose—but he prefers instead to sketch out the emotions released by the subject of his work, letting us feel as well as see, stimulating our imagination with the details he does share: those spots of color and incomplete shapes. When captured together, the result is seen to have acquired a new meaning, a hidden sensation, and this is true also for action and movement.

If the impressionist painter, or later the expressionist or cubist, has understood that they depict the emotions and essences exuded by people, events, and places, leaving exact realism to photography, then the poet must

94

likewise understand that his own choice of verses and words assembled to depict an action scene will have to express something different from fiction. Fiction doesn't aim to squeeze the quintessence from only a few words; it acts instead as a portrait, a mirror. The poet must follow a certain temporal and dynamic line and lead the reader towards something broader in different times and ways. The action can be part of the poem if structured as a sequence of images, of details each framed from a different angle. To give an example (returning again to Stalingrad), let's imagine we want to describe a scene where citizens are throwing Molotov cocktails against the German panzers lined up in a snow-covered city street. In composing this action scene, we would of course like to show the reaction of the German soldiers. The poet, with his special cameras and zoom lenses, will frame the tracks of the tanks, showing how they rotate and churn the snow to mud. Perhaps there is also blood, or a corpse on the side of the road (a dark element to add) that seems to be watching, its still eyes open as the enemy vehicles parade. We then change the shot and focus on a girl. She bites her lip; her hands shake as she holds the Molotov cocktail, ready to light it. Another sequence follows: the blue, Aryan eyes of a soldier on the panzer turret gunner. Its long black barrel rotates towards the windows to the right and left of that alley. In one window he sees the face of his wife; he is afraid of dying and never returning home. Inaction through thoughts, or hallucinations. Then the action is triggered. A Russian soldier, dressed in a heavy grey coat, throws himself in front of the first vehicle in line, forcing it to stop. We zoom in on his frozen hands. He clutches a stick as a weapon. The German machinegun roars. The snow darkens with blood. The alley window—where the soldier on the turret imagined his wife—shatters (he will never see her again) in a slow-motion cascade of broken glass that turns her into the Molotov cocktail thrown by the girl who bit her lip. There are shots in the background, a glimpse of the girl's bleeding mouth. An explosion throws the soldier on the turret from the vehicle. He lands beside the corpse, its eyes still open. Now they both seem to be watching the line of panzers in the burning alley.

This is an example of how to set up an action scene with frames of both action and inaction, some of them recurring, which can be written in verse.

To close this article, I include one of my poems from the previously mentioned *WAR* collection. Entitled *'Iraqi Sunset'* and set in Baghdad, it describes the emotions of an Iraqi woman who lost her child in a bomb explosion in a city market.

Iraqi Sunset

There are thin towers here,
of ivory and smoke,
and golden and yellowish domes
on the edge of the horizon;
I see mosques, the breasts of death
camped out between the mines,
and a fat sun, there in the middle
covered with the ruined orange fabric
of the tattered, gasping day.

My gaze starts to race
across the empty rooftops,
like a cat with the tail on fire;
it wants to join, with a leap into the void,
those flocks of mosquitoes
and helicopters with their steel, green leather
and a star attached to the belly
—the only one you can see here—
which are buzzing in the sky
alive with clothes hanging out to dry
and old iridescent carpets
stained with blood.

I close my eyes, imagining to fly
above that city, which can't tell
the living from the dead,
imagining to breast-feeding
the nacre ghost of my baby
—not the only one you can see here—
swallowed by a bomb crater
on the navel of an old fruit market.

This Is Not a Poem

Cynthia Pelayo

I've always believed that a poem should sing.

I'm not specifically looking for a sonnet with its stanzas or even a quatrain, or a haiku with its structured set of syllables, a ballad or villanelle with its set number of lines. There are concrete poems that form a particular shape across the screen or page. We have an epigram beaming with wit or satire. An elegy, which serves its purpose in mourning. We also have an epitaph, which is in a sense an elegy in miniature. We have odes that address or honor a person, place or thing, and there are other poetic forms and structures, many of them following a formula based on the number of lines, stanzas, meters, rhymes, or syllables organized by a framework in a series of beats.

But I don't want to follow formula.

I don't want any of us to follow any structure with regards to poetry if we don't want to, especially when that poem is meant to communicate something urgent we all need to know right now.

I've always believed the artist should be a rebel, someone who challenges rules and conventions in order to find the path to create something truly moving and revolutionary. Therefore, I personally reject rules designated by someone else based on how I should create art, on how I should construct a poem. As a woman of color, I feel it is important to set my own path as an artist and a poet. I write using freeform poetry, which is the rejection of any poetic structural organization. I've always been of the opinion that rules set before me were created by individuals who did not expect or want someone who looks or speaks like me to create art. Especially when talking about poetry, dark, speculative poetry that is sometimes written from a position of pain, sorrow, and panic, I feel as though any order is restrictive when emotion must take priority.

There is no formula in suffering.

We suffer, many times unexpectedly because of disease, violence, injustice, poverty and more. There should be no rules dictating how those feelings should be communicated because navigating pain is complex, it's deep, and we have to allow ourselves the freedom to explore with words how complex emotions should be expressed. So, how do we go about that? Burn it down. No one should dictate to me, or you, how an artist, how a poet should create, how we should paint words across a page that screams our hopes, our dreams, our pain, and the terrors that many of us experience daily.

The poet needs freedom.

The poet should not be limited by a number of words, or structural rules put in place by some societal or artistic construct that was likely created by a group of people who believed the arts should be exclusively created by a select few only to then be consumed solely by a similarly exclusive group. For the purposes of identification, these select few will be referred to for the remainder of this discussion as the privileged.

Now, we first need to identify the space of the privileged with relation to poetry. Historically, what type of poetry did the privileged see as value and in turn consume? These would generally be works related to beauty, whether with regards to landscapes or individuals or concepts. These are often the works that were taught in schools and used as examples of what "good" poetry is, poems that follow structure, perhaps even a rhythmic pattern.

Yet, poetry about human suffering, about race, poverty, and social justice, well, that's been more difficult to spread and access widely. At least when I was growing up. Of course, some educational systems have included the words of Maya Angelou in their curriculum regarding poetry. Many a middle schooler has read "Still I Rise." Perhaps some have read "Harlem" often referred to as "A Dream Deferred" by Langston Hughes, but I wonder if educational systems have really deeply explored the social commentary each poet was aiming to convey in these pieces?

Poetry is a powerful tool that many have struggled to understand. Some people may also believe that poetry is inaccessible because it may look strange on the page compared to traditional prose, or they are baffled by the appearance of fragmented syntax or grammar rules that may be flexed. Some people pass on poetry believing it's bland or boring or both. Others are unsure of how to read or interpret the text before them. Should you take notice of the line breaks? The ragged right edges? When and where are the pauses? Do you take the meaning of the words literally? Or do the words hold some symbolic meaning individually, in groups or stanzas? Is the meaning of the text figurative or literal? Or is the meaning a distortion that the reader must be challenged to dissect beyond what is presented before them?

Given that many people pass on poetry because they say they are unable to comprehend its meaning, I wanted to use a piece of art as an example I'm hoping many are familiar with in order to talk about the power a few small words can have on its audience. Let's think about the famous surrealist paining "The Treachery of Images" by René Magritte. Beneath the image of the black and brown pipe, the artist included the famous words "Ceci n'est pas une pipe." Translated into English, this means "This is not a pipe," which indicates the painting of the object, while a representation of the object, is not, in fact, that actual item.

These few words create a disorienting affect. Five words make the viewer contemplate theories of existence, reality, truth, creation, and more. Even these few words, that seem benign enough, generated controversy at the time Magritte painted and presented it around 1929. People expressed their distaste of the artwork, of oil on canvass, primarily because of the five words beneath the pipe.

Magritte was vocal about the criticism he received about the painting, stressing that if he had indicated otherwise—that the reproduction was in fact itself a pipe—that he would be lying because the reproduction of the thing, was not in fact that thing. So why were people upset? Because the words made them think and question their reality? Perhaps. Yet, would the painting have been as powerful without those words? Probably not. Those five words created a strong emotional reaction in the viewer, and this is what poetry can do. Poetry can make us question existence, rules, societal guidelines, and more.

So, let's take a step back and look at Langston Hughes' "Harlem" in total:

Harlem

What happens to a dream deferred?

Does it dry up
like a raisin in the sun?
Or fester like a sore—
And then run?
Does it stink like rotten meat?
Or crust and sugar over—
like a syrupy sweet?

Maybe it just sags
like a heavy load.

Or does it explode?

First, could this be categorized as a speculative poem? I would certainly argue it could occupy that space, because first, we are presented with some gruesome imagery. We read about a raisin shriveling, sitting out on a scorching day, only to have that followed up with an infected and oozing sore, uncooked meat spotted with green, blues, yellows, perhaps dotted in parts with fuzzy mold, and finished off with the visual of crusted sugar, sweet, yet unappealing. We then conclude with the image of a weight toppling over, and we are left with this question: "Or does it explode?"

What is that heavy weight? Maybe we are the heavy mass of existence the poem speaks of. So then, what does it mean to have a dream, a want, a desire that is not achieved? What does one feel when something is not obtained, denied, or taken from them? It is heartbreak. Many of us have experienced this type of agony.

When Hughes concludes his poem with the question "Or does it explode?" the image that appears for me is an endless procession of the grim and cruel realities that many people who are not privileged have to live and experience in order to survive, of being denied opportunity because it was handed to someone else, of being rejected from reaching a goal because they were deemed unqualified because of who and what they are.

For me, those last four words in this poem are a gut punch, because I know in just those few words, from my own reality growing up in poverty in inner city Chicago, what that last question means. For me, that last question encompasses frustration, anger, and rage because of my ethnicity, gender, and socio-economic class. That last question encompasses my feelings of hopelessness and helplessness of the conditions that I was born and raised in, and from which I have worked tirelessly my entire life to seek and find value and validation from a society that constantly regards me as less than.

"A dream deferred" for someone else could mean not being able to afford food, not being able to provide adequate childcare for their child, sleeping in a cold room, not being able to get a promotion that could help one purchase a home, or not being able to pay for medical expenses. "Or does it explode?" could be the constant stream of being told they're not good enough, smart enough, beautiful enough, youthful enough, talented enough, wealthy enough, and more, to deserve a better life. It's being told no and suffering in silence and suffer in silence we do.

Poetry therefore does not have to exclusively be used to communicate beauty, sweeping landscapes, abstract concepts, or experiment with lyricism. Poetry, especially speculative poetry, can explore painful emotional states. Speculative poetry can also explore realties related to justice, race, gender, and socioeconomic status.

In her poem "The Hill We Climb," poet Amanda Gorman writes towards the end:

> "…We will rebuild, reconcile and recover
> and every known nook of our nation and
> every corner called our country,
> our people diverse and beautiful will emerge,
> battered and beautiful
> When day comes we step out of the shade,
> aflame and unafraid…"

In the above excerpt, we read about people rebuilding together. We also read that the process to rebuild is difficult leaving them "battered," but that through that exercise of recreating they were also made "beautiful." This is a gorgeous dichotomy that is explored through Gorman's powerful poetry. The imagery of beauty alongside suffering is a contrast. How can something be beautiful if suffering is required to achieve it? This imagery conjures up images of people stepping out of darkness and into light. It sounds like a final scene from a horror movie, the people emerging set ablaze…but victorious from defeating a monster.

The entire poem is social commentary about people joining together to defeat hatred. Gorman acknowledges this pain in her poem, noting that rebuilding, reconciling, and recovering can come, will come, but with wounds. This is Gorman's activism. It's her acknowledgement of the pain a diverse people will experience when confronting hate, and how in the battle towards achieving something better, suffering is inevitable.

Poetry lends itself to social activism for a few reasons. For example, there's a power in the energy of the few words written across a cardboard sign at a protest, the rhythmic chants spoken through bullhorns at public demonstrations, or in public art displays that request acknowledgement of what was wrong while demanding a means to make it right. There's an electricity in protest poetry performed on stage such as "Howl" by Allen Ginsberg. There have also been spaces created specifically for poetry as social activism such as the Nuyorican Poets Café founded by Puerto Rican artists and activists in the 1970s as a space to perform poetry, sometimes specifically pieces that addressed issues of racism, discrimination, and the Puerto Rican diaspora.

The poet exists in a position and occupies a space where they can create discomfort with just a few words. Within just a few sentences and lines, the poet can speak directly to social, economic, and political concerns, tackle activism, rail against complacency, media manipulation, and more.

The three words Black Lives Matter, for example, are poetry and social activism in action. They demand that you acknowledge the system of White supremacy that has contributed to enslavement, racial segregation, lack of opportunity, and the disproportionate murder of Black people at the hands of law enforcement. Those three words express a grim truth by expressing how a segment of our population has suffered immensely, and how they continue to suffer because there are those who continue to deny the power of those three words, and thus continue to deny the suffering of Black people.

The words Black Lives Matter forces us to sit in our discomfort in living in a system that has not only historically, but continues, to present barriers to Black people. Those three words simultaneously force us to shout that the livelihood, safety, and health of Black people is important. A poet's words are movement and power.

Poetry can also address social issues with regards to the autonomy of one's body.

Poet Elizabeth Acevedo addresses abortion in her poem "An Open Letter to the Protestors Outside The Planned Parenthood Near My Job": "You don't know my god. You and mine ain't on speaking terms."

The above excerpt generates thoughts of religion and challenges to the monotheistic concepts of a single all-knowing creator (note also the lowercase g in god). For some people, the concept of a single creator, or any creator, is supernatural or an imagined element. While to others, a single creator is the basis for their foundational beliefs. Therefore, this could fall within the space of a speculative poem while also serving as a work of social commentary.

In Mahogany L. Browne's poem "For Black and Brown Girls Gone Missing" she writes:

"Ain't no reliable narrator attached to her name. She is always ghost before ever considered missing." Browne's poetry speaks about the pressing social issue surrounding the lack of attention given to missing women of color by media and law enforcement. Local and national media often under-report cases of missing women of color. However, when certain women go missing, there's almost an overabundance of reporting. The term "missing white woman syndrome" was coined by late PBS anchor Gwen Ifill to highlight mainstream media's obsession with the coverage of missing white women and its lack of interest in covering missing women of color.

In my own poetry, I recently explored missing and murdered women. *Into the Forest and All the Way Through* is a poetry collection that explores the cases of over one hundred missing and murdered women. Below is a poem from my collection written for a Jane Doe.

Doe-Eyed
The littlest doe, doe-eyed, Jane
Doe. I want to paint your nails,
Red, but not the red that stains
Your cream-colored knit sweater
I want to play dollhouse with
You, but not the moldy, brutal
Mildewed house whose basement
You were found. I want to comb
Your hair, your beautiful hair, I
Can only imagine it was smooth
As a spider web, but only those
Insects know where your face is
Now, as that was missing when
They found, you there

Name: Jane Doe
Remains found: St. Louis, Missouri
Race: Black
Age at disappearance: 8-11
Year discovered: 1983
Case status: Unsolved
Investigating agency:
St. Louis Police Department, 314-444-0100

For each of the cases, I felt it important to include the name and demographic information as well as the investigating agency telephone number, because ultimately, I want these cases solved. I want these women, and this little girl written about above, and the other little girls I wrote about, to find justice. We as a society owe them that. I believe that a civilized society should honor and respect its citizens, and the fact that so many women go missing each year, that so many are murdered, with their cases gone cold, is barbaric. How can we say we are an advanced and civilized society if we allow our women to be brutalized, forgotten, and ignored?

Over half of the cases I discussed/wrote poems for were about women of color. While the collection falls into the category of dark, speculative or horror fiction because it explores themes such as isolation, fear, anxiety, paranoia, violence, pain, loss, and suffering, it is ultimately a true crime poetry collection intended to serve as a body of social commentary.

The commentary I was trying to make with *Into the Forest and All the Way Through* was that these women once existed, they were once valued and loved, but now they are no longer with us because someone took them from us. For many of these cases, we still do not know what happened to these women, and that is heartbreaking. I believe that in many of these cases someone is still alive who knows what happened to these women.

Into the Forest and All the Way Through was my way of adding to the discussion that missing and murdered women of color are not given the level of attention and care that White women receive in the media. Therefore, as an artist— as a poet, I knew that I could give this issue the weight and power it needed.

In all of these examples regarding social commentary, protest, and justice, poetry was used as a device to communicate pain, suffering, loss, and sometimes hope. Speculative, dark, and horror poetry is a powerful tool that can explore anxieties and the human depths of despair and tragedy all within a few words.

These poems have the power to generate intense thought, anger, rage, dialogue, and debate. These poems have the power to be analyzed in academic texts, in the media, and across the social media spectrum, and why is that? Ultimately, it's because poetry, and the poet, have the gift, or perhaps even the curse, to make us feel what we don't want to feel, but what we need to feel in order to understand the human condition. The poet should be rebellious. The poet should be a revolutionary. The poet should show us the pain we are feeling and inflicting on ourselves.

Global Reflections Within Our Fear-Lit Ink: A Study on Tradition and Community in the Poem

Bryan Thao Worra

Horror poetry is for everyone.

That being said, poets and their communities across the globe are often at different stages of including horror poems within their national traditions, let alone our shared global traditions. As an example, it's difficult for most Southeast Asians to point to ancient horror poetry or works composed as recently as the 20th century because compared to oral folktales whispered as ghost stories, these subjects weren't usually written down. We have few who we'd compare to Poe in Southeast Asia, but I have been excited to see many in recent years taking the first steps towards that distinction such as Christina Sng, Cassandra Khaw, Joyce Chng, Kristine Ong Muslim, S.P. Somtow, and others.

There are many different approaches we can take when creating horror verse. After 30 years as a Lao poet, I often collaborate on projects with other refugees around the globe, particularly those with roots in the Vietnam War and other conflicts of the mid-20th century. Having served as an executive officer of the international Science Fiction and Fantasy Poetry Association (est. 1978) for most of the 2010s, I had a distinctive vantage point to see poems submitted from across the globe in varying degrees of quality with an almost endless number of themes and techniques applied. Let me confidently assure everyone we're nowhere close to exhausting the possibilities in horror poetry. There is still ample room for our darkest imaginings and innovations. But how do we tap into that, and where might we need to approach with caution?

Every poet will find their own reason for wanting to write a horror poem. Sometimes it is intended strictly as entertainment, while other times it's as a necessary or unnecessary allegory to comment on current or historical events that still drive a trauma response in parts of the poet's community.

105

Sometimes it is a release, sometimes it is a thought exercise.

Every region of the world has traditions of creatures and beings who frighten children and more than a few adults. In Southeast Asia, such entities include the serpentine nagas and the giant nyak (more commonly known as asuras or rakshasas in other parts of the world), and a variety of entities known as phi, who have counterparts in the yokai of Japan and go by many other names. Southeast Asia is filled with a dizzying number of legends and rumors regarding weretigers, who are quite different from Western lycanthropes, and some of the monsters within our myths are one-offs who appear in only one tale, while others return time and time again, such as "the frog who eats the moon" that causes lunar eclipses. If we look deeper into the proverbs and saying of different Southeast Asian cultures, we won't have to wait long before we run into one that seems to have a darker meaning in its origins. In Laos, there's a proverb that when the water is low, ants eat the fish. When the water is high, fish eat the ants. For practiced poets, it's not too hard to turn that proverb into a scary poem.

Good horror poetry rarely comes from anyone intending to become filthy rich from its creation, but more often than not, it's coming from poets who are passionate about exploring what frightens them, sometimes for the right reasons, sometimes for the wrong reasons. That was an issue I explored in my 2013 horror verse collection *Demonstra* and many other books before and since.

In writing, we see consistently that in the end, what works, works. There was a time when the writing of Stephen King was deeply loathed by English teachers, and yet decades later his writing is now regularly taught in schools. We would do well to consider the position of Webster's Dictionary in that they don't intend to enforce present-day rules of grammar, syntax, or the meanings of words as if they are indelible, fixed things, but to instead reflect on where the English-speaking world is at the time of publication.

Poets can get a good start when we consider what we are most afraid to write and what don't we dare to write After that, the poem often walks us as close to the threshold of that dark door as possible. Will we give the readers a gentle nudge to the edge, or push them abruptly through that ink-stained portal? As writers, we ought to be conscious of what we're doing rather than being fully random in the matter.

A particular exercise for me is to visualize the body of world literature as bricks forming a vast wall. After thousands of years, there are many such bricks that cover the same ideas, the same materials. But there are surprisingly a number of holes and gaps even after centuries, and that's where I believe horror poets of any country should place their priority. In the United States (US), there was a 20th-century saying that "Only Nixon could go to China." For us, we ought to seek to write the verses only you and you alone might think of creating, rather than simply saying something any number of competent poets might eventually fill.

When we write verse with an international audience in mind, I am partial to the strength of an idea or an image first. When a poem goes into translation, invariably rhymes, meter, structural constraints, and opportunities get lost. A haiku is not just a poem with 17 syllables, and considering how many words in Japanese are polysyllabic, such an approach will have limitations.

I am often intrigued by the point at which a horror poem works, and I love searching for that point in such a verse when it is most at risk of collapsing on itself in failure. A horror poem has an opportunity to succeed by following the tenebrous traditions of verse it is rooted in, or to succeed by breaking from those pulsating traditions.

I think often of the advice I give regularly to my students: It's admirable to want to emulate the writing of Stephen King, Peter Straub, Linda D. Addison, Stephanie M. Wytovich, Ann K. Schwader, and so many others. We might well wonder what it would be like if Thomas Ligotti wrote a horrifying poem drawing upon the Filipino terror known as the Aswang, or what would happen if Joe Hill took on a sonnet set in the creaking ruins of Siem Reap before the infernal gates of Naraka open for a day. But by and large, those poems likely aren't coming, and so we're left with ourselves and this realization: We already have those writers. And what they write in their lifetimes is what they will write. But what is missing within all of this is *your* voice, and what happens when *you* write to the outermost darkest edges of your imagination? Will it transform worlds as a warning or a beacon?

A good horror poem will be a bit of a time traveler. Its relevance may come and go, resurfacing when it is needed most in a distant age, occasionally retreating into obscurity until it is needed once again, and sometimes the reason it is valued may change: The mention of a vampiric Aswang in one decade may terrify knowing readers in Manila and the US, but in another, it may become a rallying symbol of Filipino identity. The Greek legend of Medusa in recent years has taken on such a change, where our sympathies have shifted to view her as a bit of an anti-heroine who was just trying to do her thing before a petulant god cursed her.

I would certainly strive to remember the Confucian principle: "Wisdom begins when you call things by their proper names," as we don't need to romanize excessively for comprehension now with Southeast Asian horror poetry. For example, there was a time when vampyr and nosferatu weren't in the common vocabulary. Poets should ideally refer to beings with correct differentiation: A river dragon isn't the same as a naga. A kinnaly is not an Asian harpy any more than pho is ramen or Vietnamese spaghettios.

Our verse should never be content merely creating a redundant understanding of a given sinister scenario or an entity from our past. Why compose a superfluous poem that merely repeats the attributes of our ancestral terrors established by prior poets? So often, a horror poem will succeed when it can achieve its effect of dread, that subtle shiver and show us a fiend where we least expected them. Perhaps this happens in an unusual time, in a place typically forbidden to them, or maybe it's during an encounter with a new culture, a new piece of technology, or something we don't typically associate with them. In my poem, "A Discussion of Monsters," we have a piece written by a Lao poet resettled in the US reflecting on ghosts of Taiwan, such as the jiangshi hopping spirits and other entities. The poem hints at Lucifer of the Christian tradition, aliens, and immigrants in the US, as well as a variety of special-effects heavy horror films created largely after the 1980s when computers became more available. It achieves this within a particular economy of words:

A Discussion of Monsters

In America, monsters arrive
Through Ellis Island,
Or from the stars,
Or morning's rogue angels.

In Asia, the ghosts hop,
Hair long, eyes black

And girls from Taiwan will squeal in terror
At that lonely world

But laugh with disdain
At Hollywood's soulless, piles of pixels and latex
Signifying obsolete demons.

One of the considerations I gave to this poem throughout its creation was that prose often demands we be very exacting and specific while poetry can traffic in the ambiguous and less explicit to achieve its effects, i.e., the sense of something lurking beneath the surface of the text.

We're writing poems, not phone books, so we have to economize and usually leave out baroque world building. That's often more liberating than you might imagine. A horror poet operates within a particular paradox: What you create is unlikely to tip the Earth, let alone the multiverse, off its axis. And yet, with just three lines about a frog splashing into a pond beneath the moon, the Japanese poet Basho created a love for the haiku form that led to thousands of translations of his poem for centuries, and today, whole conventions and lifelong friendships have formed, all from a little bit of ink.

We can't write expecting a certain result, but we must also appreciate how much just a little bit of ink could change.

At the risk of vastly oversimplifying the literary idea of magical realism for the purposes of this essay, it has often been remarked that magical realism makes the magical seem every day, and the everyday seem magical. This is not an easy feat in prose, let alone poetry. I mention this idea because we may apply a similar premise to horror poetics, especially abroad.

What is of interest to horror poets is how we might approach it practically when dealing with monsters and situations of international origin. A horror writer in any form—prose, theater, film, comics, poetry, or the like—must always look at the objects and elements of the mundane world and consider how they might convert them into the root or into an element of terrifying expression.

For example, how might we instill a sense of fear in, say, a road sign? Is it in an unusual position or color? Is there ominous graffiti, a vague warning scrawled on it? Is it embedded in the skull of an innocent or a not-so-innocent? Might it be dangling precariously from a tree or window like a gruesome guillotine awaiting an order from beyond? Is it a landmark or part of a boundary to a realm wise mortals dare not cross? There are a thousand possibilities, and similar questions might be asked of a character's favorite meal, a loved one, an old toy, a saltshaker, or even a box of half-used crayons.

Conversely, how does one make the supernatural cause or symptom/evidence in a story plausible? While a writer may take any number of liberties with a story, imaginary beings and forces, especially those of a horrific and malign nature, must often be depicted with an element of realism that accounts for why they don't simply infest or manifest 24 hours a day, 7 days a week. Creating internally consistent limitations for horrors from beyond or within is challenging enough within prose and most narrative forms, but within poetry and its economy of words there is an even greater challenge, but often a great opportunity, too, for a determined writer.

If we look at the raven of Edgar Allan Poe's famed poem, we can see several techniques used to quickly establish the peculiar circumstances that make the raven extraordinary, both in origin and mysterious, ambiguous purpose. Ogden Nash's classic poem "The Wendigo" is just 25 lines and with a handful of words manages a comedic yet terrifying, and largely accurate account of carnivorous horror adding innovations no other oral histories and traditional accounts include all while deftly positioning the reader as the next victim of the Wendigo. Is it the last word on the Wendigo? Certainly not. See the poem "Windigo" by Louise Erdrich, for example. But it is decidedly difficult for anyone familiar with the poem not to forever after at least give it some consideration in any conversation about the entity.

In Nash's "The Wendigo," the poet plays with image, sound, humor and pattern. Divided into two sections, in the first half of the poem he quickly but efficiently establishes the nature of this carnivorous forest spirit for those who are unfamiliar with it, using colors such as indigo and yellowish, which is interesting because it asserts a particular ambiguity and mystery for the reader. This is a poem that calls out to be read aloud with descriptor words practically oozing off of the page, such as "slithery and scummy," or "...blubbery,/ And smacky/ Sucky/ Rubbery!" For as horrifying as the beast is, the rhymes are wonderfully tempting to say aloud because they're likely uncommon in an everyday conversation for readers. Nash puts his own take on the creature, traditionally associated with the forest by making reference to tentacles, almost never found on land-dwelling animals. When I read this poem, I take note that the first half is spare, with most lines only one-word long, creating a visual effect of "emaciation" or hunger. Then, in the second half, the lines start to "fill up" as we talk about the monster who ate the poet's friend. The Wendigo was seen in Canada the night before but tonight is right next to the reader as Nash deftly pivots and now makes references to "you," and implies that you have just been devoured by the poem's end. Another poem one might compare this to is Ishmael Reed's 1970 classic "Beware: Do Not Read This Poem," which shifts from telling an eerie tale to one directly involving the reader being pulled into a poem, then concludes with a mention of statistics on missing persons that implies the reader has just joined them. Louise Erdrich's approach is to open her poem "Windigo" with a brief preface on the creature, then presents the poem from the first-person perspective of the Windigo directly addressing the reader and informing them of their fate and how the reader came into that situation in the first place. Interestingly, Erdrich includes a note at the beginning of how some stopped the Windigo in the past by pouring boiling lard down its throat. Is that enough to help the current reader? One might debate, as the narrative unfolds. Both poems address the Wendigo, and a poet might take interest that both approaches are effective, with enough opportunities for other interpretations.

In my poems "Zombuddha" I was cognizant of the transgressive nature of my propositions in this poem. Historically there are few poems in Asia that try to do a somewhat serious take on the intersections between Buddhist thought and the values of non-attachment in a post-apocalyptic world overrun by zombies.

Zombuddha

Utters "om," not "brains".

Is not attached to the body.
Is not attached to the mind.

Decay is one aspect of the cycle
Of birth, life, death, rebirth, redeath.
Never perfumes or gilds the self.

Comes back for you.
Perhaps right behind you.

"Keep going," he says, in his own way.

Observes a walking meditation.
Does not hurry, or drive cars or trucks.
Or tanks, or gunships or warplanes.

Will not touch money or liquor,
Is beyond the vices of lust and greed.
Focused.
Not one possession of the past matters.

Old names are useless.

Accepts every moment with equanimity.
No fear. No pain. No anger. No jealousy.
Burn him. Cut him. Shoot him. Flee him.
Free him.
It is the same.

The old riddle still applies:
"Meeting the Buddha on the road,
You can say nothing to him,
You cannot remain silent.
What do you do?"

You will destroy him to be comfortable.

Some will follow his path,
Become one with him,
Laughing at the dancing bones of zen,

The lessons of an uncertain universe.

Does a poem gain literary merit if we are intentional and thoughtful in our transgressive, perhaps heretical or blasphemous takes on a given subject? In India, Hanuman is often considered a divine demigod, revered for his prowess as a warrior and his unshakable loyalty as one of the vanara beast-men. In certain regions, women cannot enter his shrines because it is believed his powerful masculine energy will bring woe. But beyond the borders of India, Hanuman took on different significance in different nations that came upon his myth. In many parts of Southeast Asia, he is seen as a powerful, comedic cross between a simian Rambo and Casanova, filled with many deep character flaws, to say the least. But given these two very different takes on Hanuman, what happens when a poet writes about a futuristic or alternate history version of him in a country where members of both societies are present, but the legend itself is not particularly dominant? Does such a horrifying poem become heresy, or does it suggest a new way for a community to understand itself and its relationship to conflict and other social values?

This is a matter of some debate, one I would propose benefits from appreciating such questions on a case-by-case basis or a continuum rather than a binary yes/no model. A poem and by extension, its creator, ought to be afforded certain benefits of the doubt despite the considerable talent or lack thereof that may become an issue in consequential conversations in a given society. Sometimes the spaghetti sticks to the wall; sometimes it does not. Regardless, we keep creating.

In poetry, there is a possibility within language where we engage in an act of trust with the reader to create a meaning for themselves based on context. For example, Milton was a prominent poet who survived the civil wars of his country, and turned to writing verse for comfort, including his classic *Paradise Lost*. What I've always found striking about his journey as a poet is that he used many existing English words with great proficiency, yet he was also not afraid to create new words such as pandemonium, infuriate, terrific, dismissive, and debauchery to meet the needs of particular sections of his verse. In time, each poet will find their own comfort levels with what they want to innovate and contribute to their languages and others, but I hope this serves as a reminder that such a possibility of contribution is not impossible, and we ought to relish such opportunities when they present themselves.

In a world of Sharknados and conger chowders, Grecian urns, red wheelbarrows and croaking frogs by moonlit ponds, there's simply no telling what verse will catch fire and change your cosmos and the shadows of those stars.

Dare fearlessly.

Of Poison Doors and Uncarved Stones: Myth as A Means to Mystery & Ecstasy in Speculative Poetry

Saba Syed Razvi, PhD

The petal plucked from dreaming, a mystery beyond us breathing life into our beaten days: myth is the haunting of something felt beyond the singular moment of time, the experience of the otherworldly, split open into the staccato beat of syntax. It is a door of poison that, in opening, loosens you from one world into another, or becomes a path you must carve through the wilderness to civilize the senses with stone. In poetry, it is an evocation of the real and a reminder that what is alive wasn't always dead and will not stay that way.

You don't write a poem without the poem also writing you. As such, the poem unfolds in being, begins to be as it unravels you. Myth is a coming forth into light from darkness, an enveloping of the darkness within. Myth is the reminder of mystery that thrums in all things. And the poem that invokes the energetic thread of mythology is woven with as much mystery as a mastery of naming. The poem is a naming of things, and a thing of names, a spell to call down the divine, a hymn to release it, a ritual to understand, and a riddle to twist it. How you use myth in poetry is by letting it bloom within you and letting it burst forth.

Myth implies that some experience or feeling had so much intensity that it left a permanent mark. It implies that experience can have the kind of depth that will haunt the things that move forward. Human desire involves curiosity and discovery. People have an intrinsic desire to encounter things that are beyond the ordinary, and this search for mystery is sometimes seen as spiritual or religious, but always comes back to some longing that can be codified by the syntaxes of mythology. The stories about how human experiences influence the way the entire world and its seasons actually happen implies that there can be an experience of life that isn't superficial, that isn't trivial, and that has lasting consequences. Everybody wants to be

114

immortal. Everybody wants to be a mystery. There is something of that in the use of mythology, inherited or invented, in our writing.

We know the world through the ego, through the structures we have created within our lives, through the active observation of experiences. But we feel the world through instinct and impression, through the shadow self, through the passive revelry of association and sensation of all the elements we have experienced and stored in the unconscious spaces and which we recall through the conscious mind. Myth is a way to connect those ways of being, knowing, and feeling. So, in a poem, the use of myth has the capacity to invoke deep resonance, to invite a conversation with tradition, heritage, and the cultural consciousness that makes up the world around us, situating our impressions with a meaningful matrix. And using myth in poems involves honoring the mystery and mysticism of that which is not tangible in the specific materiality of that which is tangible. Engaging with myth in poetry asks us to explore the archetypes of the unconscious and the structures of the ego, delighting the senses we define and those that we cannot quite pin into place but compel us through desire, curiosity, abandon, and rapturous frenzy.

In these kinds of poems, we don't seek to make it impose an abstract sense upon an instinctual impression, but to envelop ourselves in something that transcends us, something that reminds us of what is unbound to the earth and what is ecstatically open to the eternal sense of the cosmos. What is it about the heart nebula that reminds us of the intimacy of love, or the demotion of Pluto that stings of the abandonment of death? What of the turning of the seasons reminds us of the possibilities unfolding on the path, or the convoluted wisdom of the crone hard won through roots and thorns, through the cycles of moon and spring? The path ahead is made by both seeker and guide, and the poem uses its utterances to shape both syntax and sensation as it brings the reader into the experience shared by the poet.

Considerations of Approaching Myth in the Contemporary Experience

Myth is a way of connecting to what's beyond the ordinary. Poetry, too, is a way of connecting to something both within and beyond the moment, so there is an inherent synthesis in the generative capacity of these modes of expression. It's a desire for depth and resonance beyond the immediacy of the moment. Speculative Literature is already invested in exploring ideas through indirect means, using cognitive dissonance to inspire reflection and observation in a way that disarmed vulnerability and delight can do best.

Myth connects the reader by creating connection to that space of wonder, uncertainty, or possibility.

There are many ways to incorporate myth into poetry, but in speculative literature, the approach to mystery and ecstasy can intertwine many of the emotions and insights that readers come to expect with literature that are surreal enough to illuminate our nightmares, staunch enough to open our throats to wonder, strange enough to imagine a technique of possibility. When poetry slips just beside the sublime and the grotesque, expanding its approach to the experience of the moment, it invokes the myth of human heritage and hope. There are as many ways into myth as there are ways into a story, a song, or a sensation, but the following approaches are those I favor in my own expression. My interest in the mythic is a connection to the cosmic and the fundamental, the mystery that moves us forward and the ecstasy that fixes us in place, all held within the nebulous matrix of the collective consciousness of humanity. In those echoes, we find our own lives take on a significance and a radiance, a primacy like the contralto to the ephemerally mortal.

One works myth into poems by way of the choreography of empathy and the gestures of compassion, by finding a sameness in the difference that can bridge the divide between the parts of the psyche. A mere reference or categorical exploration of the mythical can still point the reader toward that space of deep connection to the lineage of humanity, but a deliberate and figurative interpolation of the phenomenon by which we witness and declare our immediacy will invite the reader into that space completely. We can be immersed in shadow or erased by light, we can delineate the ages of our own chronologies or trace the taxonomies of our ambitions, and all are ways of bringing myth and mystery into poetry.

Our contemporary world is so driven by technology and commerce, by motion for the sake of some ultimately empty productive sense of progress, that myth can be a remedy for the robotification of the human spirit. In these times of technological dominion, we are perhaps as removed from a sense of personal power as the ancients were—and, so, an approach to the world that seeks both understanding and comfort, both reason and release from burden, can sometimes answer the unyielding anxiety of observation, or things waiting to be bought or sold. The ritual of the wolf and the witch, the creative fire of risk and curiosity, all demand an investment in some aspect of the self that develops through quest or chance, not commodity, not just the call to business or order.

Using myth in poems automatically moves beyond the solipsistic, connecting us to the human lineage and heritage, to the moving and breathing longing for rich experience. Of course, a good poem itself is an invocation of experience, not just a retelling or representation. In that way, myth as a structure of thought can create an aperture or opening into poetry that accesses a dimensionality of feeling, a multiplicity of perception, fusing the horror with bliss, braiding anxiety with anticipation, even bringing significance to the play of shadow and light that connects the world of ideas and their passage into the potential of the future. Mythopoesis, myth as a structure of thought, is a conceptual entrance into the use of myth in poetry. It invites us to an immersion of feeling and thought that speaks to deep attentiveness, liveliness. Just talking about ancient myth, even in a topical or allusive or referential way, can tap into that headspace, but it isn't enough of a consideration alone if one is to write poetry that seeks a mystery or ecstasy of expression. The mythic approach demands a relinquishing of commodity and reciprocity, speaking instead to the sacred and sacrificial, the risk of loss and self in whatever is found.

Because our world has different cultural norms, relative to the ancient world in which myth developed, we must find the nexus between contemporary and ancient approaches to cultural expression and literacy in order to locate a site for psychosocial expression. Deliberate attention to techniques can be tailored to suit these overlapping ideas, especially when revitalizing sensory impressions.

When you use myth in writing, sound matters—aural texture envelops us, prosody steadies us. Unlike the image, fixed in place and filed away for later inspection, sonic elements are immediate, implying movement and connection across time and experience. For myth to work in a poem, it must feel timeless— or at least suspended outside of the linear shuffle of time. The mythic gesture invites sensation by way of prosody—a wet and fecund loam for a blooming metaphor, or a dry and brittle, soft and sweet breeze for some metonymy across lexical dreamscapes—words not linked to the metronome of philosophy, but carried in the cadence of dance, the meter of song. World-building matters. The sound moves us by way of something other than an abstract logic, moves us at a primal level. In a poem, we expect to feel carried away by this frenzy to feel the wisdom of the ancients. This can be achieved through lexical play with innovative formal structures, or it can weave through alliteration, consonance, repetition and rhyme, anaphora of gesture, or echo of refrain. Mood and atmosphere matter, much in the same way as a stage, a station.

In the ancient world, where myth was born, humans had more of a relationship to the natural world—and to the world of the strange that in its literature wasn't so fixed but was fixated on immediacy. Much existed in the oral dimensions, so sound took experiential priority over image. Sound has now to reinvigorate the image for us in a world that is conscious of literate and image-focused tendencies, which enable passivity and by which immediacy has been replaced. Bringing together the fixed locus of the image and the immediacy of the present in the aural dimension enables us to layer a sense of mythic significance to the everyday language that appeals to readers of poetry on the page.

Considerations of Myth as Process

What exactly is myth or mythology or mythopoesis and how does it relate to poetry at all? Determining these things can help us make sense of what to do with myth-work in speculative poetry. More than one answer exists, and how we choose to define this impulse in our writing influences how we use it and to what end.

The broadest way to describe myth might simply be to say that it is a kind of narrative rooted in a worldview and materiality that seeks to transcend ordinary explanations of phenomenon beyond our control. In the ancient world, when human experience was seen as less removed from the natural world, at least in literature, this often involved cosmogonies about the world's origins or those of people or seasons. In the modern world, mythopoeia has involved creating new myths that take into account the archetypes suggested by the ancient world and our views of it. We understand our place in the world by looking at the stories of people before us and the hopes they have for what lies ahead. The human impulse to seek comfort in something beyond the self is sometimes seen as a religious impulse, sometimes seen as a faith in scientific principles, sometimes seen as an interest in esoterica or magic or even the reliable uncertainty of the natural world unspoiled by the hands of humankind.

When we turn to poetry out of a sense of powerlessness or lack of control, there can be a comfort in the approach of myth in those poems. When we reach for poetry out of a maelstrom of emotion, it can be a steadying gesture to think of the matrix surrounding us in which those emotions exist. I think that we turn to myth in order to find comfort, to find belonging, and to feel a sense of wonder and delight that is often lost in the mechanization of our experiences in the mundane world. Reaching out to the mythic impulse is a way to reach for an immortality tinted with the brilliance of glory or for a resilience as alive as the blooms of spring after winter.

By fixing our own experiences into the spaces reserved for awe or endlessness, we can find a way to make our senseless moments take on meaning. For this reason, I think that the most effective contemporary poems that engage myth are the ones that take on more than just reference, the ones that engage with a multiplicity of poetic elements.

In recent years, we find ourselves again in the season of the witch. More appropriately, we are in a season of esoteric possibility, collaborative and feminist power, mystical and ecstatic appeal, and ecological awareness. Magic is a mode by which we may process our relationship to the world— and the mythic allows the exploration of a magical or metaphysical aspect of the psyche without tying our actions in the artwork to the function of collective action at the expense of individual agency. The mythic is, then, a function of how our present moment comes to matter to us on an individual level, while reminding us of our collective experience and histories.

Rituals of divination that have become so popular in recent years remind us not only of the knowledge that can be ascertained by deep, indirect reflection, but that the old ways of knowing things, ways rooted in the matriarchal, the feminist, and the sacred are not relegated only to the dry catalogue of the Hermit's pages, but are also available through the ecology of the sage and the celebration of the harvest, through the revelation of the feast and the whimsy of the dreamer at rest. Scholars have reminded us that the old stories bear signs to guide the way, that all experiences are a kind of sacred palimpsest.

Poetry's value is that it is not utilitarian in nature; so, the knowledges blooming within the expanse of poetry is subjective in nature, valid for various individuals in various manners. When the psyche's archetypes and shadows interact with the indeterminate nature of ontological domains, the rule of seasons and floods yield as much resonance as the orbits of the celestial, bringing the immediacy of experience into a sense of multidimensional vibration.

Tarot cards are one of the ways in which contemporary divination practices open avenues for the experience of the psyche; they are an interesting way to think about the relationship between reader and poet, especially as it relates to the poet's approach in creating a terrain of the poetic matrix for the forays of the reader. By imagining this and other related approaches, we can see how myth can find its way into the speculative reader's particular attention, a fusion of cartomancy and cartography, one waiting for inductive approach to map out potential and one acting on deductive approaches for the decoding of symbols —a balance of active and passive mechanisms for epistemological experience.

Poetry demands attention as a vessel bearing the cargo of experience. Poetry uses myth to navigate mystery, invoking the immanent, opening into the ineffable. Imagine the poet as The Wheel of Fortune. The world opens and reveals a turning wheel of woven light, petals plucked from dreaming fall to planets, roses bloom over the cosmos. The universe invites the mind into an experience of invocation, of one into all ones. We use myth in poems when we want to connect to a transcendence, when we seek some portal to the mysterious beyond the mundane order of the self.

Poetry demands attention to the spaces between knowledge and utterance. When longing is a cartography drawing the eyes in and calling out the cadence of experience, myth is the emblem that calls us beyond the texture of sound, inviting a liminal dimension, a threshold between the roots and the reach. Imagine the poet as The Seven of Cups. Through the sounds of words, we find a terrain, a world we walk through while we follow the light of the stars. The sound of the worlds is the sound of words on an astral plane, an experience both fixed and fleeting. We use the sounds that ground the body in its materiality, sounds and cadences enough to taste, lush enough to savor. We drink from their cups. Intoxicated on sound, we look for meaning in the enveloping of otherworldliness. Myth becomes a bridge of the senses. We seek what could be beyond.

Poetry demands a pain of pleasure, a price for its prosody, an obstacle for conquer. The mystery breaches sense of self and possibility. Imagine the poet as The Eight of Swords. The thicket traps the majesty of the swan and holds the flurry of the hummingbird. In the thicket, thorns become swords, thorns become roses. What span of winged majesty can slip into the frenzied beat of color and beak and blood in the thicket: the swan's breadth or the hummingbird's epiphanic bursts? And which struggle speaks to the psyche, to the psyche's shadow when both blood and roses bloom? What collapses and restrains us, frees us. Poetry uses myth to make meaning of struggle. Any cage is a calling, a wall opening into a garden, a thorn to beckon the release of a bud of blood. We use myth to celebrate the prowess of possibility. The cavern, glowing, says we are the big and also the small we seek within.

Poetry uses myth to build a structure of understanding a potency that can navigate mystery and endure the confrontation. Imagine the poet as The Nine of Wands. The Call of beast and herd moves in a dance of harmony. What is the order out of the chaos that surges forth and calls to the power latent in every breath? Is it the battle cry of the body, or the surge of the burden bonded with bestial harmony that propels the quest? Is it the syntax or its refrain that moves us? The pattern of one shape ties to the heritage of all shapes, and language is haunted by the marks left behind. We charge with the power of the echoes that drive us. Every shape a wand of rhabdomancy divining momentum. Myth in poems makes a linage of every vessel, every shape bearing the weight of those cast before.

Poems demand the speaker's immersion, and though myth is the matrix of creation, where the quest yields light and the fall yields thrill, where the sound calls forth a blush of blood, and the opening sends a release from the self, in the poem, the vessel breaks open. Imagine the poet as The Fool. Unfurling, open, unrooted, and flailing and falling and flying, aloft in the ether of light and psyche, in the ribbons of harness and hesitation. The seeker is a sage when he abandons the path, when she relinquishes reward for the risk of rapture. The poet is a seeker, and myth is a path to letting go. Myth yields an experience of the ecstatic in poetry. It leaves the speaker suspended in discovery beyond the aims of the quest that inspired the seeking.

Myth in poetry is a courtship of mystery. The poem asks us to experience an oubliette of awakening, to let go into a place enclosed. It isn't a letting go into the nothing that generates fear of uncertainty. It is a whirl of the ecstatic that unravels us. It is the vision of the hanged man, suspended upside-down, resting in a moment of uncertainty.

Considerations in Using Poetic Elements
in Order to Create a Passage in Tune with the Mythic

We invoke mystery and transcendence through an approach to the mystical mindset. We use atmosphere and mood, excluding what doesn't fit and repurposing what does. We remember in a way that removes us from the telling and places us into what is told.

We choreograph a longing for that mystery to suspend us in a flirtation between hope and despair. The sound and cadence must belittle and beckon us. The sonic texture of the lexical choices must vary in ways that create a disruptive velocity of music.

We make meaning of the struggle through an order that suffocates. We use mystery to pull us into the doubt of the psyche, the trap of the obvious. And we use prosody to create an order in and through the line, as a thing against which to struggle. It is both a trap and a means to the center of the labyrinthine, the restraint that enables the wild and uncontrolled release of the senses from control.

We use structure to make mystery a heritage, a haunting of every step that makes the singularity of the subject matter. If every poem is in conversation with all of poetry, then every structure is haunted with echoes. Myth makes every story an echo of sacred time, a being infused with the spectrality of timelessness. Each structure chosen or rejected reminds us of the tradition and rebellion of logic, the curiosity that compels us and the search that demands forgetting.

The poem triangulates the speaker and the listener within an arena made of Chronos and Kairos. The speaker's role is one of suspension. The listener's is one of acquiescence. Or, sometimes, the other way around. The poem unravels itself into the matrix of the mysterious, both arriving at and leaving behind an awareness of certainty. The choice lets the reader and the poet into the conversation, making possible an opening: as above, so below; as without, so within.

Poetry that uses myth at its core steals a flash of the visionary, the mantic dreaming of Cassandra or the delicacy of Ishtar's rage—a suspension of limits: expanse into the everlasting garden of timeless possibility and the pit beneath that roots it. The mythic is more than just an experience of the ordinary, and the poem that uses it seeks to weave that which exists outside of human capacity into the utterances that shape our reaches into language and syntax. By the poem's engagement with sacred ritual or esoteric resonance, with rebellion against and continuity with tradition, the poem reminds us that every ordinary pattern bears an echo of glory, the fire of the cosmos and the kiss of the chthonic. Like a door of poison opening into vision shielded in shadow, the impulse of the mythic kills us (or a part of our observation) to carry us forward; and like paths cut through wild gardens, it leads us on stones into the darkness shadowing what is carved with our inner light. Any poem that embraces myth must remind us of this suspension of self along the spectrum of the limitless.

Consider a Prompt to Try:

Begin by writing in belligerent prose about an account of an experience that you cannot put into ordinary words or sense. Think of something you may have been through that you just couldn't describe in normal conversation with others and in everyday language. Be extra. Use a decadent pen and paper without lines. Write in solitude and silence without attention to the clock. Then, remove, by striking out, any references to ordinary logic or explanation. Replace them with some detail of that sense that you were trying to explain that particularly symbolizes that sense to you. Consider this Version 1.

When you are done, edit the passage four separate times, with the following idea in mind for each revision:

- Select a pattern of cadence or a sound palette to use in the poem's words and lexical choices. On a separate piece of paper, rewrite Version 1 and bring the words into alignment with your linguistic filter. This is now version 2.

- Select a prosody or pattern of rhythm that accentuates the struggle between intensity of experience and inadequacy of the language of ordinary speech in which to render it. On a separate piece of paper, rewrite Version 2 and bring it into alignment with this metrical filter. You may change the arrangement of lines to suit the prosody. This is now Version 3.

- Select a structure and shape for the poem that you think suits the word sounds and line patterns, one that creates for you a spectrum between the pain of longing in an experience of the mysterious and the release of self in an experience of ecstasy. On a separate piece of paper, rewrite Version 3 so that you align it with your imposition of structural choices. You might discover shifts in your lexical choices or your prosody, and this is the place to consider formal strategies so that you are in conversation with the ideas and literature that brings echoes into your creative process. This is now Version 4.

Imagine the echoes in the psyche of the seeker, whether that is you the poet, a figure in the poem you are creating, or some imagined reader. Understand the quest or the puzzle at the core of the poem, something that animates its momentum. Use the context of the world of your experiences, the world of the texts you've referenced, the active and passive processes of understanding that you are using, and the aims of symbols in reaching the reader. On a separate sheet of paper, rewrite Version 4 so that you bring into alignment the echoes within the whole poem at every level that remind you of the most intense aspects of the initial experience you referenced and the challenges you faced in expressing it. Let this be the poem—and go on to as many drafts as you wish, before you call it complete.

By turning the initial experience through the revolutions of these poetic elements and considerations, you re bringing the ordinary into the realm of the marvelous. You are deranging its path to the senses to create flourishes of possibility.

You are mything the mundane.

A Note on the Setting of the Type

From within the crocodile's keep,
I have emptied myself hollow—
I am left.
              With the echo
of you,
    your words left.

          Split me open
with a drop of sound
                like a spike,
slither in an open cave,
    a desert of nothing but snow.
Leave me—
    brittle,
Bare and bonestrung—
              a lute.
Leave me to long—
Is my heart a stone
        or, a geode—
filled with stones,
          candy-hued crystalline teeth,
prismed, longing
        to reflect the light
left,
    instead
        of holding its echo?

Into the Dark Woods: Fairy Tale Poetry

Carina Bissett

Once upon a time there was an apple, a mirror, a key, a ring, a rose, a witch, a wolf, a cottage, a crown. And in that faraway land, just past the dark forest, live beautiful princesses, hero girls, talking animals, brave tailors, and beastly bridegrooms—all fated to live happily ever after. The evil queens, ugly stepsisters, sly wolves, stupid ogres, and crippled dwarves get what's coming to them. Or so the stories go.

Yet there is a darker side to fairy tale, a realm under the hill where silver trees bear jeweled fruit and masked dancers trace the patterns of an enchanted faery reel. In these stories, Sleeping Beauty wakes to twins suckling at her breasts, Donkeyskin flees from a father's unnatural lust, Cinderella's stepsisters are mutilated and then blinded, the Little Mermaid's tongue is cut from her mouth, Little Red Riding Hood slips into bed with the wolf, and Bluebeard hoards his murdered wives in the cellar. The narratives here are not for children, nor were they ever meant to be.

These pieces of oral folklore are also known as old wives' tales, cautionary stories treading the line between wisdom and folly. They are yarns threaded with advice on ways to navigate the dangers of the world. It wasn't until much later that these fragments and fables were collected, predominantly by men, who polished off the rough edges and shaped them into fictions suitable for children. It is those shiny, sanitized tales that so many readers are familiar with today.

So, what is a fairy tale? According to folklore scholar Marina Warner, fairy tales are not easy to define. They slip into "folk tales" from the oral tradition; they diverge from popular notions of individual narratives; they connect to the past with familiar characters, plots, and images; and they contain symbolic language and recurrent motifs to create a visceral reaction in the reader. "Fairy tales are one-dimensional, depthless, abstract, and sparse; their characteristic manner is matter-of-fact—describing a wolf devouring a young girl, ordering a palace chef to cook a young woman, or chopping up a child to make blood pudding arouses no cry of protest or horror from the teller," writes Warner in *Once Upon a Time: A Short History of Fairy Tale*; "This is as it is, as it happened; the tale is as it is, no more no less."

The earliest stories crossed back and forth between folk tale and myth. In fact, the classic myth of "Cupid and Psyche," which appears in *The Golden Ass* (a novel by Lucius Apuleius from the 2ⁿᵈ century AD), resonates in shape and form with the Norwegian fairy tale "East of the Sun and West of the Moon," the titular story of the Scandinavian collection published by Peter Christen Asbjørnsen and Jørgen Moe (1843–44). The influence of this Greek myth can also be seen in other variations of the animal bridegroom motif such as *Beauty and the Beast* (1740), which was written Gabrielle-Suzanne Barbot de Villeneuve, a member of 17th-century French salons. A 2016 study published by *Royal Society Open Science*, "Comparative phylogenetic analyses uncover the ancient roots of Indo-European folktales" by Sara Graca da Silva and Jamshid J. Tehrani, backs up this theory of transmission. For instance, their research shows that "Beauty and the Beast" is one of the oldest stories known to mankind. It's this transformative ability that continues to make fairy tales fertile ground for contemporary reflection. By nature, the mutability of these "wonder tales" offers countless variations for writers to explore nuanced expression and experience.

In the second half of the 19th century, American folklorist Francis James Child anthologized 305 traditional ballads from England and Scotland in the ten-volume opus *The English and Scottish Popular Ballads* (1882–98). This collection of folk songs is colloquially known as the Child Ballads, and like the Grimm Brothers fairy tales, they record stories of murder and monsters, grief and guilt, brides and beasts. This examination of song only supports the foundation of fairy tales in poetry. For instance, the Child Ballads include "Tam Lin" (Child 39), a familiar story about a mortal man rescued by his lover from the Faerie Queen. Another popular song in the index is "The Twa Sisters" (Child 10), a macabre song about sisterly rivalry, a bone harp, and retribution. This particular murder ballad has since inspired more than five hundred versions recorded in the Roud Folk Song Index. These endless variations exemplify the mutability of oral traditions and their translation to poetic forms.

"A fairy tale keeps on the move between written and spoken versions and back again. The circle loops out across the centuries, forming a community across barriers of language and nation as well as time," writes Warner; "The stories' interest isn't exhausted by repetition, reformulation, or retelling, but their pleasure gains from the endless permutations performed on the nucleus of the tale, its DNA as it were."

For instance, "Cinderella," one of the most well-known fairy tales of all time, has been recorded in the fairy tale canon as far back as 9th century China. Yet Tuan Ch'eng Shih, the scribe who recorded the text of "Yeh-hsien," indicates that this Cinderella tale type was old even then. A few of the motifs in this Chinese Cinderella will be familiar to Western readers: neglect and abuse by a stepmother and a stepsister, a magic helper, the gift of beautiful festival clothes, and the search for the girl who loses her shoe in the flight home. However, some of the details reflect the story's origin. In the Chinese version, the magic helper is a golden fish that continues to help even after death, and the girl's festival clothes include a cloak of kingfisher feathers and tiny golden shoes.

Several centuries after "Yeh-hsien" was first written down, another variant of Cinderella was posthumously published in *Il Pentamerone: Lo cunto de li cunti*, also known as *The Tale of Tales* (1634-36). In Giambattista Basile's "La Gatta Cenerentola," the central figure is clever and revels in trickery and immorality. In this first Western rendition, Cinderella Cat murders her first stepmother only to then be saddled with a second. This version also features a lost shoe—one of the most prominent details to dance its way through the numerous Cinderella variants that followed.

In the Jacob and Wilhelm Grimm's version "Aschenputtel" (1812), the stepmother hacks off a toe and then a heel in her efforts to force her own daughters' feet into the infamous slipper. In this variant, the stepmother and stepsisters are later blinded by the ghost of Cinderella's dead mother in bird form. This rags-to-riches story has other variations in Charles Perrault's "Cendrillon" (1697), which includes the more familiar wand-waving fairy godmother, a pumpkin coach, and cheery rat coachmen.

Sifting through fairy tale variants is one of the most useful tactics for poets searching for new avenues to examine elements of these recognizable tales. There are plenty to choose from, and the fairy tale canon continues to grow exponentially when it comes to the more well-known narratives. For example, English folklorist Marian Roalfe Cox published a collection of 345 variants of "Cinderella" in 1883. By the time Swedish folklorist Anna Birgitta Rooth tackled the Cinderella Cycle in 1951, there were more than seven hundred versions to record.

Although there are numerous volumes of fairy tales, the following are few key essential texts for enthusiasts to explore:

- Giovanni Straparola, *Le Piacevoli Notti* (1551/53)
- Giambattista Basile, *Il Pentamerone* (1634/36)
- Charles Perrault, *Les Contes de Ma Mère l'Oye* (1697)
- Madame d'Aulnoy, *Les Contes des Fées* (1697)
- Mademoiselle de la Force, *Les Contes des Contes* (1698)
- Madame de Villeneuve, *La Belle et la Bête* (1740)
- Madame de Beaumont, *Beauty and the Beast & Other Classic French Fairy Tales* (1756)
- Jacob and Wilhelm Grimm, *Die Kinder und Hausmärchen* (1812/15)
- Hans Christian Andersen, *Eventyr* (1835)
- Peter Christen Asbjørnsen and Jørgen Moe, *East of the Sun and West of the Moon* (1843-44/52)
- Alexander Afanasev, *Russian Fairy Tales* (1855/67)
- Thomas Frederick Crane, *Italian Popular Tales* (1885)
- Oscar Wilde, *The Happy Prince and Other Tales* (1888)
- Andrew Lang, *The Blue Fairy Book* (1889)
- Joseph Jacobs, *English Fairy Tales* (1890)
- L. Frank Baum, *American Fairy Tales* (1901)

Many of these can be found in the public domain. Others, such as the tales by Basile and d'Aulnoy, can be read in their entirety in translated collections.

Although the stories in the Andrew Langs' series of "coloured" fairy books were curated and sanitized for a child audience, the twelve volumes in the series are easily accessible online and contain a wide array of fairy tales from around the world. Andrew Lang and his wife Leonora Blanche Alleyne, known by friends and family as Nora, published this popular collection over the course of two decades, starting with *The Blue Fairy Book* and ending with *The Lilac Fairy Book*. Several of the fairy tales included in these volumes mark their first appearance in English.

However, no discussion about fairy tale poetry would be complete without a mention of Anne Sexton's indelible contribution to the genre with the publication of *Transformations*, which contains seventeen retellings drawn from the Brothers Grimm including "Snow White and the Seven Dwarfs," "Rumpelstiltskin," "Rapunzel," "Cinderella," "Red Riding Hood," and "Briar Rose (Sleeping Beauty)." The obscure tale "The Golden Key" closes *Grimm's Fairy Tales*, so perhaps it's unsurprising that this is the story Sexton uses to open *Transformations*: "The speaker in this case / is a middle-aged witch, me— / tangled on my two great arms, / my face in a book / and my mouth open wide, / ready to tell you a story or two." These poems take on a contemporary tone with mundane references to the modern world. Snow White has cheeks "as fragile as cigarette paper"; Iron Hans is transformed "[w]ithout Thorazine / or the benefit of psychotherapy"; and Cinderella's rags-to-riches is echoed in a tale of a nursemaid who lands an heir: "From diapers to Dior. / That story" (Sexton). She spins new life into these familiar yarns. She makes them her own.

Another pivotal collection that laid the groundwork for fairy tale poetry is *The World's Wife* by Carol Ann Duffy. These themed poems draw from fairy tales and myth in a feminist exploration of gender roles and the treatment of women in mythical, folkloric, and historical contexts. Duffy subverts stereotypes with a poetic voice that ranges from dramatic monologue to balladesque authority. She urges readers to re-examine cultural conventions and preconceived expectations. When the wolf steps on the path, the girl will surely follow. But why? Duffy explains the motivation behind the decision in "Little Red-Cap": "Here's why. Poetry / The wolf, I knew, would lead me deep into the woods / Away from home, to a dark tangled thorny place / Lit by the eyes of owls." For this is where the transformation begins.

The interest in fairy tale poetry steadily grew in the early 2000s, which can be seen in *The Journal of Mythic Arts* (1998-2008), curated online by folklorist, author, and editor Terri Windling. This selection of fairy tale and mythic poetry includes work by such luminaries as Neil Gaiman, Holly Black, Charles de Lint, Margaret Atwood, Veronica Schanoes, Mario Milosevic, Jeannine Hall Gailey, and Theodora Goss. In his poem "Instructions," Neil Gaiman guides newcomers through the gate to Faerie: "Remember: that giants sleep too soundly; that/ witches are often betrayed by their appetites; / dragons have one soft spot, somewhere, always; / hearts can be well-hidden, / and you betray them with your tongue." And perhaps it's those prohibitions that make fairy tales such rich material to mine in the first place.

Also featured in the *Journal of Mythic Arts*, Jeannine Hall Gailey looks at fairy tales through a feminist lens, and many of these poems ended up in *Becoming the Villainess*. Hall Gailey is unapologetic as she strips away the veneer from tired tropes ranging from classic mother-daughter conflict to the image of beautiful dead girls. Readers eavesdrop on the mundane and the magical as Hall Gailey explores the inevitable transformation from hero girl to wicked witch.

Fast forward a decade, and Instapoet Nikita Gill takes this a step further in *Fierce Fairytales: Poems & Stories to Stir Your Soul*. A quick glance at the poems' titles reveals the slant of Gill's feminist reimagings: "Why Tinkerbell Quit Anger Management," "Lessons in Surviving Long-term Abuse," "Two Misunderstood Stepsisters," "How You Save Yourself," and "Take Back Your Fairytale." Gill celebrates witches and crones. She subverts gendered stereotypes. And she encourages self-empowerment. "Await no princes to save you / through their lips touching yours / whilst you are in unwilling slumber," Gill urges to the classic cut-out characters Snow White and Sleeping Beauty; "Darkling magic is coursing through those veins, / turn it into kindling, my resourceful girls, / find one another in the fog realm, / *wake each other up instead.*"

Not only are these fairy tale poems being published, but they are winning awards. Theodora Goss collected eight stories and twenty-three poems in *Snow White Learns Witchcraft*, which won the 2020 Mythopoeic Fantasy Award for Adult Literature. Christina Sng is a two-time Bram Stoker award-winning poet of *A Collection of Nightmares* and *A Collection of Dreamscapes*. Poems centered on fairy tales and myth continue to receive acclaim and interest. Like so much of the world around us, these wonder tales often defy prediction or logic while remaining rooted deep in the collective unconscious. These tales provide a wealth of material that can be stripped, pummeled, reassembled, and yet still retain a sense of familiarity that keeps readers returning for more.

In *Seven Miles of Steel Thistles: Reflections on Fairy Tales*, scholar and author Katherine Langrish writes about the enduring popularity of fairy tales:

> They've been told and retold, loved and laughed at, by generation after generation because they are of the people, by the people, for the people. The world of fairy tales is one in which the pain and deprivation, bad luck and hard work of ordinary folk can be alleviated by a chance meeting, by luck, by courtesy, courage and quick wits—and by the occasional miracle. The world of fairy tales is not so very different from ours. It *is* ours.

In the highly acclaimed *Paris Review* column Happily, poet and author Sabrina Orah Mark uses fairy tales to focus her contemplations of motherhood and life in general:

> The reason why fairy tales last is because they allow us to

gaze at ourselves through a glass that is at once transparent and reflective. They give us a double gaze to see ourselves from the inside out and the outside in, and they exaggerate our roles just enough to bring into focus the little pieces of monster that grow on our hearts.

Once you are ready to incorporate a fairy tale into your own work, there are a few things to consider. Before you even pick up the pen, it's important to spend some time with your fairy tale of choice. Start by identifying the Aarne–Thompson–Uther (ATU) tale type. This catalogue of folktale types was originally composed by German folklorist Antti Aarne in 1910. It was revised and translated into English by Stith Thompson (1928, 1961) and again in 2004 by Hans-Jörg Uther. Although it is geared towards scholarly categorizations, it can be a handy tool for writers seeking a deeper understanding of fairy tales and their connections to other stories in the canon. For instance, "Cinderella" can be found under ATU 510: Cinderella or Cap o' Rushes, which has two sub-categories: ATU 510A: Persecuted Heroine and ATU 510B: Unnatural Love. This shows a connection in the variations of "Cinderella" and "Donkeyskin," which opens new avenues to explore.

The next step is to take a closer look at the central elements of the tale type. The ATU Index is often used in tandem with Stith Thompson's Motif-Index of Folk-Literature, which is more commonly known as Thompson's Motif-Index. Thompson, who also worked on the ATU Index, defines these motifs or granular elements of folklore as "the smallest element in a tale having a power to persist in tradition." These elements must be unusual, which therefore makes them memorable. For example, the motif might be magical objects, or ghosts and revenants, or otherworldly journeys. By identifying the central characteristics of your chosen fairy tale, you will then be able to brainstorm connections that might not have occurred otherwise.

Once you've identified the ATU tale type and the central motifs, it's time to dig into the ways other writers have approached the story. Who else has retold your selection, and what angle(s) did they explore? Look at older variants as well as contemporary retellings. At this point, you might also want to explore scholarly articles and artistic interpretations of your selected piece. How have the perceptions of story changed over the centuries? Has it been retold on stage or in song? How have artists approached the material in visual representations? Once you are armed with the knowledge of the tale's history, subtext, and meaning, you will be able to engage with the elements that intrigued you in the first place. You'll discover your own "Happily Ever After."

Exercises:

- **Rework the Plot:** Select a fairy tale that really rubs you the wrong way. Do you hate it when the Little Mermaid gives up the chance to regain her natural form? Do you wince when Karen's desire to wear red shoes results in amputation? Do you loathe the sisterly rivalry in "Cinderella"? Good. Change it. Let the mermaid's knife fall. Let Karen keep her shoes. Let Cinderella and her stepsisters work to protect each other. Rewrite the plot so the story's trajectory takes a different path—the more unpredictable, the better.
- **Pick a New Point of View:** Fairy tales are often populated with villains and secondary characters who deserve the opportunity to tell their own stories. Why did the lady's maid in "The Goose Girl" step into the role of the false bride? Who built Rapunzel's tower? What does Rumpelstiltskin plan to do with that baby? The answers might not be what you first expect.
- **Explore Origin Stories:** What happens before the "Once Upon a Time"? This is your opportunity to find out. Write about the things that happened before the traditional tale starts. If you feel especially daring, you can combine this prompt with the point-of-view of the villain or a secondary character. Where did the Evil Queen in "Snow White" learn witchcraft? Was the wolf in "Little Red Riding Hood" once a man? How did the Pied Piper acquire his flute? Start writing and find out.
- **Consider Imagery & Symbolism:** Fairy tales are often brimming with interesting images that can be explored through symbolism. They can also be connected with similar motifs and symbols in other fairy tales and myths. For instance, a poisoned apple plays an integral role in "Snow White"; golden apples are jealously guarded in the Garden of the Hesperides; and then there is the infamous Apple of Discord. These objects—keys, mirrors, birds, spinning wheels, apples, shoes, snakes—often come with outside associations. Sticking with the symbolism of the world's most famous fruit, you might discover that an apple cut on its hemisphere will reveal the seeds arrayed in a pentagram. Is it any

wonder an apple might become a tool utilized by a witch? Your challenge is to weave these symbols into your work through cross-pollination.

- **Change the Setting and/or Genre:** What happens if you retell "The Twelve Dancing Princesses" set in an underground nightclub during Prohibition? What if "Beauty and the Beast" happened on a space station? Setting and genre both provide new avenues for retellings. You can explore your favorite time and place. Look for historical periods or futuristic possibilities that might align or enhance your selected tale's themes, symbols, and motifs. The same goes for genre. If you want to be daring, select two disparate genres and see what happens.

- **Mash It Up:** Take two fairy tales and/or myths (or a combination of the two) and find a connection. Is there a way you can seamlessly blend the themes, motifs, and/or symbols? Or can you take the other route and play up their differences? Is there a character you can move from one story to another? Can the characters from one tale be transported to the setting of the other? The only caution with this exercise is to resist the urge to mash more than two or three tales. Too many elements and you risk losing dramatic impact.

- **Consider Personal and Emotional Impact:** When a fairy tale calls to you on a personal level, there is often something there waiting to be explored. Your challenge is to use the tale as a launching point to free write about your personal experiences and the ways they relate to your selected story. Treat it like an experimental prose poem or work within the constraints of form poetry. Later, you can go back and sift through the words for story seeds. You might be surprised by what you discover.

Seven Swans

Brothers dear, known only to me
   as letters carved on coffin lids,
      midnight visits and a wing's caress—

Do you think of me when drifting,
   passing by clouds and dreams long lost?
Or do you forget my vigil
   while soaring high on heaven's breath?

Bound by trials of silence I toil alone
   cradled high in these lofty gnarled arms,
      —this Middle Earth—

   not high enough to palm the moon,
      nor so low as to form clay men
         while treading upon barren shores.

By day I weave your stinging shirts
   working in sweat and skin and bone.
Binding spells of silence and hope
   with silken thread torn from my scalp,
      charmed with blood drawn from screaming fingertips.

Come night I scan starry skies for you,
   wondering.

Brothers dear, I know your desires
   but do you wonder at my needs,
      my wishes for fanciful flight?
How could I resist that dark down
   lost while you were circling overhead?

Soon you'll know the truth blood brothers,
   if you don't suspect the truth already.
One of you will live with a token wing
   in trade for time spent sewing my own shirt
      —of feathers.

Dreams as Poetry:
Translating Dreams into Verse

Joanna C. Valente

Are dreams real? Do we speculate the unknown in our dreams because we're too afraid to be vulnerable enough to do this during our waking hours?

When I write poetry, I write from my dreams, because my dreams are not only the unfiltered thoughts and images running around my brain, as if a sponge is bleeding out everything it's ever seen and experienced—but also because it is a portal into the unknown, the spiritual realm that we can tap into if we want to, if we know how to harness that energy.

I believe in dreams. I believe dreams tell us about ourselves in a way that our conscious brain doesn't, and I think it helps to process stimuli in a way that molds our perception. Part of what makes dreams so powerful is the fact that we aren't editing them. Often, writers self-edit as they write, picturing what the reader may want to hear—or what a workshop may advise them to stay away from (because all poets write about the moon for instance, and we're told to stay away from "clichés").

I abhor this.

Write what you want. But write unfiltered and unedited, at least, at first. Dreams serve as some of the best prompts or sources of inspiration because they are raw, honest, unfiltered, and unaware of social norms or constraints or rules—and most importantly, they are unconcerned with what we think or feel is interesting or subversive. When we write the unknown, we tend to focus on ghosts, the dead, or the unseen around us.

What is the known? What is the unknown? Instead of thinking in these terms, what do we consider real or unreal? What is belonging versus unbelonging? All of these ideas are related in that what we consider "real" is how we belong and fit into specific groups or ideas; for instance, the dead are seen as part of an "other," an ethereal world around us that humans can't perceive. Therefore, it is part of a realm of unbelonging, and thus, unknown and othered.

Instead of us seeing what we can't perceive as the "supernatural," we should, as writers examine it merely as another reality that is part of the natural world. There is nothing "extra" ordinary about it other than our ideas of what perception is.

Is it truly unknown just because we can't perceive it in our waking hours the same way we usually perceive the sounds of birds in the morning, cars honking, people chatting in a bar, a coffee maker hissing?

To write the unknown, we must deconstruct what we think of as "unknown" or "mysterious," and lean into our unfiltered minds—into a dreamlike state instead. Just because something is unknown to us in a particular moment doesn't mean it's mysterious or speculative in nature. What defines a moment or idea as speculative, or surreal or absurd, are the threads that tie images and moments together. How do the actions, the movements, the characters all interact? How do they coexist together?

Dreams, for instance, are absurd because the observer experiences reality without time or place as a grounding force, but rather as a detail that can be changed within an instant. You may find yourself in a dream first set in Brooklyn and then find yourself on a rock in the middle of the Pacific Ocean without boarding a plane or driving cross country. You may find yourself with the inhuman ability to fly—and yet still remain in a human body. That is the unknown—that is speculative.

For instance, Christina Rossetti's iconic poem, "Goblin Market," focuses on an entire fantastical universe humans often don't see—or come back from, at least not quite in the same way:

> "Twilight is not good for maidens;
> Should not loiter in the glen
> In the haunts of goblin men.
> Do you not remember Jeanie,
> How she met them in the moonlight,
> Took their gifts both choice and many,
> Ate their fruits and wore their flowers
> Pluck'd from bowers
> Where summer ripens at all hours?"

Then, there's H.D. who wrote about nature, and myth, so effortlessly that every world—fantasy, reality, mystical—blends together. In her poem, "Eurydice," speaking of the very liminality of life and death, and whatever is in between or after or before:

"hell is no worse,

no, nor your flowers

nor your veins of light

nor your presence,

a loss;

my hell is no worse than yours

though you pass among the flowers and speak

with the spirits above earth."

Keeping a dream journal can train your mind to remember dreams, especially if you are able to maintain a schedule of writing down your first thoughts, or the first images, that come to mind after waking. This will allow you to be more open and present in those first waking moments—but also begin to train yourself to think in a more unedited, unfiltered way when you begin the writing process.

As part of this process, I take long walks and write down any thoughts, images, feelings, or emotions I have; I am a strict documenter of each day and moment. Taking photos on walks can also help jar or propel a narrative that isn't necessarily linear or known while capturing the energy of a moment, time, or place.

The unknown is less about a story and more focused on energy. We can't easily define energy or intuition. Both energy and intuition are part of our body and mind's function to perceive reality, the real and unreal, the known and unknown.

By definition, intuition is "the ability to understand something immediately, without the need for conscious reasoning," according to Google's dictionary. Similarly, some definitions for energy are as follows (also from Google Dictionary): "a person's physical and mental powers, typically as applied to a particular task or activity" or "the property of matter and radiation which is manifest as a capacity to perform work (such as causing motion or the interaction of molecules)."

For many people who work in divination, such as tarot readers, the idea of harnessing energy and honing intuition is a large part of the craft. Tarot readers, by default, work in the realm of the unknown because they have to *read* what isn't explicitly expressed around them.

Another way to write speculative poetry is to combine dreamlike writing with ideas of the tarot, whether one uses the tarot as a prompt or not. What do you imagine the people around you are thinking and feeling? What are their hidden fears and desires? Trying to understand people's motivations and backstories broadens the writer's capacity to build creative narrative landscapes.

To do this, I sometimes will draw three cards. What are the cards saying? How can I make this a narrative? Sometimes I write a poem based on the storyline I see in the cards or use the cards as characters and the spread becomes the motivations, fears, wants, needs, and overall narrative of the poetic thread and plot.

Essentially, working with narrative—within a nonlinear framework of the past, present, and future—can help form a speculative poem. Blending time together creates an absurd, surreal portrait of a moment, person, or place that itself becomes as unknown as it is known. This duality is created by both the sense of familiarity of a narrative and setting—but is foiled by the nonlinear storytelling that mimics a dreamlike landscape in that the events may not make logical sense or may appear randomized or bizarre.

When taken out of a linear narrative, anything can become unknown and strange—as if we are looking into a mirror—and in that mirror isn't our face but someone else's. It is both familiar and unfamiliar—a new unknown.

I've done this in my own work; for example, in the "Marys of the Sea," the title poem from one of my books, the experience deals with my sexual assault and the subsequent trauma. However, many of the images and narrative come straight from a dream I had around the time I was writing the book, and emotionally processing what happened to me as a form of shadow work and therapy. These images came to me subconsciously, and by delving into them deeper, and threading together a narrative, I was able to more closely understand my own pain—and thus, empower myself.

What makes something haunted, for instance, isn't the idea that someone has died and is now a ghost, sometimes appearing before us or moving objects around unexplained, but the idea that we can't control it. We cannot edit it into something neat and tidy. So, just as we need to write more automatically, we also need to undo the idea that everything has an explanation or a neat ending.

Of course, to do this, it can be helpful to use music as a way to turn off your "editor's mind" and allow yourself to write without worry. I often write to classical or jazz, using the rhythm as a meditative and reflective technique. Like many writers, I tend to overthink every word, and this allows me to tap into my subconscious mind more freely.

Most dreams, for instance, end without a resolution or closure. That is the ultimate mystery and unknown. Take everything you know and throw it out the window. Leave your poem out in the moonlight, put it in a glass bowl, and then take it out. What words can you make out? How did the moon and the water change the poem, for instance?

Write the poem as you would—and then leave it for three days. After three days, take out the ending. Or maybe make the end the beginning, and the beginning the end. Rewrite the poem from another point of view. Write the poem from the perspective of something undead. What are ways you can change or reorder time—or rewind reality?

These are the questions I ask myself when I sit down to write a poem, or when I think about what I don't know—which is honestly everything. It's merely about the order and understanding to leave out the logical steps to the hows or whys. Just let the image and the moment be itself, without explanation or closure.

It's vulnerable to write truthfully, badly, nakedly. It's vulnerable to write in a way that we haven't been taught—and if anything, may be the opposite of our education. It's vulnerable to present ourselves in an untidy fashion. Sometimes, however, it's exactly what we need to do when we go off to explore the unknown—to explore our dreams.

The Woman Who Dressed in Gold

& the Greek man with the bad
exhaust yells out his car
window, everyone is a monster
sometimes.

False reality
forms under layers of rock
on Greenpoint Ave

leaks into the water & you become bullshit
versions of yourself—
layers and layers of boneless
threads

sticking together with the fear
others will discover
you are a shell of someone

cooler and better, an invention
from a bot programmed
to please;

God's in the algorithm
So feed it

$$$

& the stopping
of your body

into blurry angels or
sunsets that

even

con men fall in love
with.

This time, it was with none of us.
Not even the con man could
con himself into
real love

or a body like
God's body

and God's body is like our body.

We are made up of lines and lines
go on forever.

I Got My Passport Stamped in Hades: Waking the Dead in the Poem

Leza Cantoral

My husband and I were ready to move from New Hampshire to Upstate New York. Zillow became my millennial pornography. Eventually we found the perfect place. It was affordable, small, cute, and had tons of character. Built in 1890, it sat upon a hill, minutes from downtown Troy, NY near Albany, and this craftsman bungalow with beautiful pebble stonework on the porch and fireplace was calling my name.

On the night before our house inspection, I dreamt vividly and lucidly of a woman. She appeared out of the blue, materializing like the Cheshire Cat. There she was, looking directly at me with piercing eye contact and a strange smile upon her lips, part amused, part excited, just beaming with arcane knowledge.

I began to scream. I felt like I was seeing a ghost. But she continued smiling her cagey Mona Lisa smile as I screamed bloody murder, her expression unwavering, her demeanor unchanged by my reaction Finally, patience worn thin, she remarked, quietly but firmly, "Are you done? Because I need to show you something."

You can bet that stopped me dead cold. I regained my composure through sheer shock as she handed me a book. I noted the details with fascination. Who was this mysterious woman and why did she care if I listened to her?

The book was hardcover, vintage, with a pale teal and soft grey dust jacket. I made a great effort to read and remember the title: *The Absence of Memory*. Once I had read and re-read the looping Victorian cursive font, I wrote it down in my phone notes within the dream itself to be sure I did not forget. Upon waking, I promptly wrote it in my real iPhone. I could not get back to sleep because I still felt her in the room, sitting in the corner, watching me for the duration of the night.

When I awoke, I messaged a friend who was also equally curious about the mystical and strange, and told them about my dream. I discovered they had conjured the Greek goddess Fortuna that very night by lighting an amber scented beeswax candle they had made by hand while reciting an incantation to wish me good luck at our house inspection. The strangeness, however, was just beginning. A week after my dream, they, too, had a dream where I came to meet them at a bar holding the very book the mysterious woman had given to me. They opened it, and upon the first page it read:

EX LIBRIS
HAZEL I. DREW

We googled the name, and to our surprise, we found that she was a young woman who had been murdered at the tender age of 20 years old, not far from where we were moving. She had worked as a governess for a professor at Rensselaer Polytechnic college, a 10-minute walk from our future house. Troy was the town she lived and worked in, often riding the train down to NYC, up to Albany, Boston and even Providence, RI and Salem, MA. She was killed in 1908. She was quite an adventurous and bold young thing, exploring all that upstate New York had to offer as she bounced from house to house in the employ of various prominent members of the Troy government.

We also discovered that she had been the original muse of writer Mark Frost for the character of Laura Palmer in David Lynch's cult TV show *Twin Peaks*. The fact that she had already served as a muse for another writer, and so recently, was probably the strangest aspect of it all. Mark Frost grew up in the area and his grandmother would tell him the woods were haunted with the ghost of Hazel Drew. During a Twin Peaks reunion at the College of Southern California, the television series' co-creator, Mark Frost, mentioned that Hazel's story came to him by way of his grandmother, Betty Calhoun. "I'd heard stories about (Hazel) all through my growing up, because she's supposedly haunted this area of the lake. So that's kind of where Laura Palmer came from," he said.

Once I moved, my friend came and we set out to find her grave and learn everything we could about her, including her connection to our house. The burning questions were: Why was she killed? Who killed her? What threat could a 20-year-old girl pose to anyone? Especially one that warranted her being killed in cold blood with a rock to the back of the head only to be left to bruise and bloat at the bottom of a popular meeting place for young lovers called Teal's Pond, up in Sand Lake.

When we went to the graveyard, we could not find her. We combed through the cemetery for about 20 minutes, at which point I walked to the back and approached a tree that had caught my eye when I first entered. It was a towering ominous thing with gravestones leaned up against it all around. I reached out and laid my hand against the tree. I rested it there for a solid minute, feeling nothing. Upon removing it, I was startled by a sharp pain shooting through my hand, and it was sharp enough that I shook it out, muttering to myself as my friend approached me, "I shouldn't have done that."

"What?" they asked.

"I shouldn't have touched this tree. Now my hand hurts," I replied, still shaking it out, baffled by the persistent stinging sensation (no it was not poison ivy). It felt like I had stuck my fingers in a light socket. Like I had gotten electrocuted. My friend, being the sensible person they are, walked around to the other side of the tree and touched it.

They began to gag and cough.

"I think I am gonna be sick!" they yelled.

"What?" I said back.

"I said I think I'm gonna be sick!" they yelled again, stumbling away from the tree as they continued to double over, gagging and retching and coughing.

I was confused and concerned, but I didn't really know what to do. I didn't want them to vomit on me, so I kept my distance but watched closely as they stumbled through three rows of graves only to eventually collapse upon one, knees to the ground crunching in the snow in exhaustion.

Then, there was another yell.

"I found her!"

"What?"

"I found her! She's here!"

And I'll be damned, but the grave they rested their weary hands upon was none other than the grave of Hazel Drew herself. Our mystery girl had finally revealed herself in true dramatic fashion. My friend finally stopped gagging and I raced to meet them. As I approached the grave, I began to feel a light tapping at the back of my head. At first it was barely noticeable, but it got heavier and more insistent until I could no longer ignore it.

I heard a voice yelling in my mind, "Like this! Like this!" I turned around and saw her floating behind me in a white flowing gown, her long blonde hair blowing in the wind, her eyes afire as an electric blue-green halo surrounded her while she approached and seamlessly entered me.

As her icy body merged with mine, I felt phantom blows against my head, felt waves of her fear and confusion as a man tackled her from behind, her face pushed down and beaten upon the lush grass until she was dead.

Such betrayal.

Such blindsight.

I heard a second voice then, a suave male voice calling out jauntily, "Hello, beautiful!"

I saw his loose-fitting tan spring suit as he approached, his bowler hat, his moustache, his brown hair and brown eyes. I asked my friend if they heard that.

"A man?" they asked.

"Yes," I replied. "He's saying *hello beautiful*."

"I can hear that!" my friend exclaimed, stunned. They described the murder as they saw it play out: Hazel with her straw hat and hat pin laying upon the ground nearby, her hair up in a bun. The beating and the eventual rolling of her lifeless body into the pond.

Wide eyed and speechless, we could do nothing but witness her tragedy on repeat. We left the graveyard shaken and dazed before arriving at a local diner. As we waited for our food, we heard a waitress walking by ask "Is Hazel coming?" as if it was the most ordinary thing in the world. Her lips did not move, but her voice was clear as day. Fully and thoroughly spooked, we wrapped up the day with some heavy drinking back at my house where we mulled over the events. We especially sensed her presence in the only bedroom with an original closet door.

A door with an elegant antique keyhole.

My friend had found an antique key on the ground at the Charter Street Cemetery by the Witches Memorial in Salem, MA on an earlier trip and had brought it with them with the intent of using it for a conjuring ritual to summon Hazel. They had tried it in other doors with no success, but to our utter bewilderment, it actually fit when we tried it on my door.

By the end of their visit, we realized we could not leave this case untouched and that we were fully committed to getting to the bottom of why Hazel ended up at the bottom of that pond. I did not know why Hazel wanted me specifically, why she had laid out her life at my feet, but my heart went out to her. My obsession with tragic women had a history after all, beginning with Marilyn Monroe, then Sylvia Plath, both of whom I studied for years, trying to return to the moment of their deaths, to feel what they must have felt in those final moments, betrayed by those that they loved most.

I dedicated that bedroom Hazel's room, since that is where we felt her presence the strongest. I painted the walls a deep indigo blue. I dyed my hair blue as well, compelled by a mad urge to undo the months of perfecting my dusty peach. This was the dawning of quarantine, and as the world shut down, I spent more and more time in my haunted house. I made her an altar, and she would make requests for books she wanted to read and offerings that would please her. I learned she was especially fond of fresh roses, peaches, and jewelry. I did my best to oblige because happy ghost happy house, right?

Based on what I learned from communing with Hazel and with other spirits and entities such as Baron Samedi and Santa Muerte, I came up with a concept for a workshop I could do via Zoom. The goal was to try out a series of exercises that would conjure and channel a spirit to help with a piece of writing. Merging my two loves, magic and writing, it began with an incantation and an offer of an exchange, something like a bad habit or a vice one could give up, alongside a physical offering to the spirit. Then we summoned the spirits by candlelight and allowed them to enter us and write through us.

The exercises yielded fascinating and diverse results. Some students conjured divine entities, some called on spirits of the departed, someone even conjured a demon. Many of the students described an altered perception with their mind going blank or even a sudden download of new information and inspiration when they wrote in their ritual space. They told me the things they wrote were in new voices they had never before seen or heard.

Through working with spirits like Santa Muerte and the ghost of Hazel Drew, I learned that it is not that hard to summon a spirit (though not always advisable) as long as you have pure intent and an offering they deem suitable. Spirits want respect. They live a strange existence in between realms. They have freedom of movement but lack the one thing we have—a body. Essentially, we have access to the one realm they no longer do.

Some people get a high from working with spirits. I am one of those people. Since I could remember, I was fascinated by all things dark. Being in the presence of death gives me a jolt of adrenaline that changes the way I see things. It turns up the colors, sharpens my senses. I think spirits sense these kinds of people and are drawn toward them. They want to be seen. After all, what is the fun of haunting a skeptic who will chalk your words and deeds up to mundane explanations instead of actually listening to your story?

I started writing poetry in my teens to deal with depression, teenage hormones, and the confusing twists and turns of intimacy. Young love. Young angst. Altered states. Poetry felt like the closest art form to music or painting. Poetry somehow bypassed the constrictions of prose. Poetry gave me the freedom to voice the hard-to-articulate turmoil I felt as I shifted from childhood to adulthood. As I began to explore my witchy side, Sylvia Plath, along with some of the French Symbolist and Surrealist poets like Baudelaire and Rimbaud, mystics like W.B. Yates and Aleister Crowley, unlocked new dreams for me. I began to see poetry as not simply a way to express myself and self soothe but as a way to actively conjure forces into my life.

The first time I felt a connection to someone dead through poetry was when I read Sylvia Plath's *Ariel* collection. Her voice rose from beyond the grave with such a chilling vibrancy that it felt as real as someone alive, screaming into my ear. I re-read that collection so many times that it began to possess my own voice. That was the first time that I felt anything akin to channeling the dead. Her imagery seeped into my imagery, her short clipped visceral lines, her beautiful righteous rage and passion for life. The bee poems especially compelled me. I started hearing bees buzzing and smelling honey. I even wrote a few of my own bee-inspired poems.

When Hazel came into my life it was a similar degree of intensity. She had no writings I could study, but the circumstances of her life as we unfolded them, along with the vivid visions and conversations I had with her, gave me a picture of the girl she once and still sort of was. She would pop into my head when I played certain music, saw certain colors, walked down certain streets of downtown Troy.

Poetry gradually became a way for me to explore characters and worlds beyond myself. To channel the voices of the dead who no longer had mouths to speak. I wrote the following poem while sitting on the banks of Lake George, which I later came to find was Hazel's anticipated destination when she was murdered. She planned to board *The Mohican* on its virgin voyage around Lake George for the 4th of July weekend. I wrote it contemplating her tragic fate, trying once again to put myself in her shoes, to feel the simple joy and anticipation she must have felt at the prospect of riding a ferryboat for the very first time in her life. Looking into the lake, I thought of her and let myself slip back into her time and her headspace to the moment before her life ended.

In lore throughout the world, vengeful ghosts return to harm and haunt their murderers. Whether or not Hazel haunted her killer after her death, I cannot say, but I do know she wants her murder solved once and for all. I chose to listen to her, to fight for her truth to be heard, and to use my words to share her story.

Growing up in Mexico I witnessed the celebrations of the Day of the Dead firsthand. On November 1st, when the veil is thin, people pay homage to their dearly departed, laying out their favorite foods and drinks. Popular offerings are hard liquor, cigars, sugar skulls, and fruit. Things to tempt them back to our mortal realm. A party to let them know they are not forgotten. This is the greatest honor you can bestow on a spirit. The ritual of remembering battles the corrosive absence of memory that is the ravages of time.

I am not sure if we conjured Hazel or if she conjured us. We are linked now forever. I have a muse and she got a vessel to the mortal realm, a mouthpiece for her story. The strange energies unlocked when I touched that tree in the graveyard have reverberated through my life ever since, much like the wood that vibrates from the blows of an axe. I got my passport stamped in Hades. I can never go back to the way things were before I touched the tree of the dead and learned the tragic tale of Hazel Irene Drew.

Untitled

She never made it
To Lake George

She did not board
The Mohican

She put on
The outfit he wanted

She came
To the spot he said

A rock
To the head

Instead of a kiss
A death

On repeat
While she waits

By the tree
To tell of how he did it

Like this, like this!
She screams

By the lightning / struck tree
Blackened, twisted portal

Into her realm—
Her telegraph pole

To receive messages
From minds

Of mortals
Seeking glimpses

Of a world unseen but felt
Like the lightning & the rock

A kiss from a ghost
An icy bite

From her lips
To yours

Historical Horror in Poetry

Sara Tantlinger

Horror has always existed within the chronicles of history. Ranging between books that draw inspiration from Vlad the Impaler or Countess Elizabeth Báthory, to more current trending true crime podcasts, the bleak and bloodied footprints, figures, and events from history hold undeniable appeal to horror writers. After all, how many times have we read a news article only to think, "you can't make this stuff up." Sometimes reality is indeed stranger and darker than fiction.

As poets, especially, using such inspiration for our stanzas presents unique challenges. When it comes to writing a short story or a novel, writers generally have more time to incorporate historical details. Even with a longer poem, there are only so many specifics a verse can hold before it becomes bogged down and the poem's rhythm runs the risk of getting too muddled. The aim of using historical horror within poetry is not to show off every minute detail of research you've learned, but rather to transport the reader into the world you've crafted within a short frame of time. A few strong details as opposed to a large checklist of items goes a long way in constructing the imagery and mood contained within a poem.

Research offers the opportunity to take the tiresome adage "write what you know" and instead, make strides to learn what you want to know. It is easy, however, to get lost in the research. While the exploration into the past is a crucial step, and perhaps often the first step taken for this particular subgenre of writing, it's important to remember to resurface from the rabbit hole of research and to actually write. It can be helpful to give yourself a time limit. For example, research your subject for 20 minutes and then write. If you're missing some important piece of crucial material, go back and research for another 10 minutes and then write again. Finding what process works for you might take some time, but it's worth it to have limits so you don't spiral down into all research and no writing.

In terms of historical horror, a poem is like a postcard sent from the time period you're writing in. What details, images, emotions, and phrases are you going to craft on your postcard? What kind of journey do you want the reader to go on with you? Figure out what you need to know and what you want to write about, and take the steps needed to feel comfortable writing about that subject. You didn't live during 1890, so try not to get hung up on the tiny details of the name of the manufacturer who provided the glass for a window in a certain city and so on. I tend to hope and believe readers are a little more forgiving and willing to suspend their disbelief if small particulars like that are not perfectly accurate. You're telling a story through poetry, not providing a historian's account of an event.

History is just history until we decide how we want to bring it to life within our writing. For horror, we know it's important to emphasize the atmosphere, dread, and tension, but it's also essential to have some heart to the story, and with poetry, we tend to take the ink of that heart and bleed it everywhere. With *Cradleland of Parasites,* my collection inspired by the Black Death and other diseases, I took my time to research horrific accounts such as Daniel Defoe's *A Journal of the Plague Year*, the "bills of mortality" postings, which showed an increase in plague victims weekly, and a few descriptive passages by Welsh poet Jeuan Gethin, who died from the plague himself. I used these materials to study what people witnessed happening to each other in dark alleys and poor farmlands as plague ravaged entire families. From there, I created characters within the poems. I could have only written about the plagues themselves, but featuring real people like Princess Joan of England, who died from the plague during travels for her planned betrothal, added a layer of heartbreak to the poem. The wedding never happened, and by capturing the devastation the disease left and how Joan's death shattered her father, I was able to use real snippets from history to highlight true horrors suffered by the rich and poor alike. Other characters in the poems are fictional ones I created, but their sorrow was inspired by true accounts of how the Black Death brought such great fright and ruin. Adding vulnerable humanity into the verses greatly contributed to those snapshots of the past breathing their own stories right onto the page.

With a single poem, you really have to narrow down the focus of the postcard, but you also have the chance to use as much or as little of the research that you want. With a collection as opposed to a single poem, it's helpful to think of the arc the collection will go through. Where will the collection take the readers from start to finish? Will it exclusively focus on one time period, or will there be changes with time, characters, and other viewpoints?

When I tackled infamous serial killer H.H. Holmes in *The Devil's Dreamland,* I knew I wanted my collection to transport the reader back into the late 19th century as we witnessed Holmes' escalation from conman to murderer. The collection begins with an overview poem that introduces readers to Holmes and to the metamorphosis the book aspires to reveal to readers. From there, readers journey along from the birth of the killer, to his days as a young man and medical student, his arrival in Chicago (as seen in the poem accompanying this essay), all the way to his final moments before execution. The setup for that particular project helped make the collection accessible to those who may not read a ton of poetry. It's easy to get lost in our own heads and in the elaborate worlds we create in poems; while I highly advocate for writers to write for themselves, when doing something like a collection inspired by historical events, it's also crucial to keep an audience in mind.

Though historical horror poetry might be a niche category, there is still a market for it. The work has the potential to reach lovers of history, true crime, horror, and those interested in your chosen subject, as well as readers who love dark poetry. For *The Devil's Dreamland,* having a timeline, character arc, and sequence of events all slowly revealed throughout the poems became beneficial in achieving a strong connection with readers of all types. Establishing that connection also stems from confidently knowing the subject well. As aforementioned, you don't need to play the role of expert historian but being comfortable in your ability to answer questions and generally talk about the chosen event or figure from history helps a great deal. There are many ways to keep organized, and we all have our different preferences. Whether you want to use colored sticky notes, an app, handwritten notes and highlighters or whatever works best for you, I do recommend having some sort of system in place to keep your research organized, especially if you're doing a longer project like a collection that relies on a lot of historical details and dates.

For *The Devil's Dreamland,* I read everything I could find about Holmes, both myth and fact. Since he left such a trail of lies behind him, many writers who tackled Holmes used their own fanciful versions to fill in those gaps of what happened, and sometimes this was passed off as nonfiction. That left me with a lot of comparison work to do in my notes, and also quite a bit of investigation to sort out what quotes Holmes actually said and where information originated. There's a quote often attributed to Holmes due to its appearance in Erik Larson's popular book *The Devil in the White City.* The quote reads, "I was born with the devil in me. I could not help the fact that I was a murderer, no more than a poet can help the inspiration to sing." I have seen this quote on shirts, internet images, in other books and more places, yet, the quote's origin seems to only be a blurry clipping from a sensationalized newspaper where any journalist could have written the words of Holmes declaring, "I was born with the devil in me."

There are instances where Holmes wrote about evil and darkness in his confessions and memoirs, but nowhere did he fully write that quote in his own musings. For me, I became obsessed with understanding how that quote got passed off in a nonfiction book, and while you don't have to spend as much time researching details like that as I did, there is a sense of satisfaction in following the clues and being able to deduce your own conclusions. This can set your work apart from others who have tackled a similar subject matter. Also, since my entire collection surrounded Holmes' life, I gave myself more time with the research than I would if it had just been a single poem. I knew the collection needed consistency in its narrative, but at the same time, I gave myself room to take the facts and twist them into the story I wanted to craft through poetry. I was also careful to include a note at the beginning of my book which explained how the collection was indeed fictional poetry inspired by history.

While reading accounts about Holmes' life, I would jot down or highlight interesting terms I came across, especially in regard to descriptions of 1890s Chicago since that was my main backdrop for the collection. Having key words in mind was helpful for getting the poems started; I enjoyed using the bits and pieces of historical details I found, but I didn't let that dictate the entire poem since I still wanted my voice and analysis of Holmes and the other points of view used to come across clearly as my own interpretation.

Point of view itself is an incredibly useful tool in all of poetry, but with historical horror, it presents the opportunity to get creative. Point of view and voice go hand-in-hand, and when it came to Holmes, I was able to read his own writing available online through the Library of Congress. Reading work written in his voice and style was invaluable. I learned how eloquent and idyllic he could paint scenes, which was fascinating and horrifying given his status as a killer. Reading his memoirs was a crucial find for me when it came to understanding how he charmed his victims. We're so lucky to have accessible documents online and in libraries. If you're able to find newspapers, journals, or other primary sources from the time period you're interested in writing about, I highly recommend taking the time to do so. Finding poetry written during that specific time period is another helpful tool. It's beneficial to see the words and phrases chosen, the preferred meter and structure, and so forth. Anyone can find the first few hits on a Google search, but not everyone takes the time to dig up the more obscure and usually more interesting details that take more effort to procure.

The fusion of learning how language was treated or structured during your chosen time period and combining it with your own writing voice presents an exciting chance to create something strong and unique. And again, because I think it's important to keep in mind so as not to overwhelm yourself, you are fusing horror and poetry and history together to create poems and a story. Don't be afraid to let ideas wander into territory far away from the actual historical events. Though, reading texts from experts on the matter or reaching out to interview them is a wonderful route to take in sharpening the viewpoint you're tackling.

Don't be afraid to get experimental with voice and points of view. For example, in *The Devil's Dreamland*, while there are of course poems told through the viewpoint of Holmes, his victims, his wives, and so forth, my poem "The Bloodletting of a New Century" is from the point of view of the time period. It's a piece that introduces how the new century hoped for optimistic change, but instead, became complicit in the creation of a serial killer. There are also poems from the viewpoint of Chicago as Holmes walked its streets and darkened many doorsteps, from the point of view of the Great Chicago Fire, and from the perspective of the infamous "Murder Castle" hotel Holmes had built. While much of what the hotel contained has become more fantasy than fact, I was able to combine both the research I found and the wild thoughts of how to make it horrific with trapdoors and acid vats in the basement into those poems, all while breathing life into an inanimate structure that would have such stories to tell.

Similarly, in *Cradleland of Parasites*, I have poems told from the point of view of diseases and historical plagues, not just from the voices of the characters I crafted. Poetry has long held fascination for me because as poets, we have the opportunity to try a myriad of techniques. Add history and horror into that mix, and the options are endless. A short story can sometimes work quite well from unusual voices and forms, but it needs to be able to hold the reader's attention for much longer. With a poem, you can experiment as much as you want on one page and try something different on the next. Specifically, with historical horror, one poem might assume the point of view of a sensationalized 17th-century French pamphlet while its companion poem is told from the view of Louis XIV or from the perspective of a bottle of wine that survived the ages and witnessed terrible calamity and so on. The opportunity to bring in darkness, get weird, and create something others might be afraid to tackle is an exciting challenge poets are uniquely suited for.

When dealing with something like a serial killer or true crime, or even the Bubonic Plague, I looked to hundreds of years ago because any victims of Holmes, for example, would no longer be around. It's something far enough removed that it didn't feel voyeuristic writing about it and adding in my own takes for a fictional collection of poetry based on history. While comfort levels may differ with every writer, I do think intent matters, and it's important to be aware how writing about historical events could have implications depending on the way you go about it. For me, it was important my collection showed Holmes as a monstrous human and did not glorify his actions. At the same time, I didn't shy away from the more gory and grotesque descriptions, so finding your own balance will be another important element.

I don't have to tell poets how crucial imagery is in their lines, but with historical horror, it becomes essential to paint those moments with all the senses you can get into your piece. While writing about the Black Death, I took my time in creating a rotting world, a place that didn't shy away from showing readers decaying, boarded-up houses while plague doctors in black masks stuffed with juniper and mint burst into those homes. I led readers through a path alongside those greedy doctors as they robbed dead villagers and burnt bodies outside at night in a scorching burial pit. All of these little historical details mixed with the horror of pushing the boundaries swirl together to flavor the poem, and thus create a horrifying postcard of memories for your reader to savor.

Some of the key points I hope you take away on your exploration of historical horror are as follows:

- Find balance between researching and writing
- Flavor the piece with authenticity, but don't get hung up on playing the role of historian
- Trust the readers to go on this journey with you back in time
- Blend research with your own voice and style of poetry writing
- Experiment with unusual points of view
- Utilize all of the senses to amplify descriptions of the past

The exciting thing about historical horror is that you get to choose what you want to write about. No one is forcing you to take an exam on the information. Your poems won't pass or fail based on how much research you do, but being comfortable with your subject and exploring new ways to hone your craft is more likely than not going to lead to some incredibly unique, macabre, and grotesquely wonderful historical horror poems.

Blood Clot Passenger

1886, late summer, early morning
a man steps off a train
thirty-five years old, five foot eight
blue eyes
striking against
miasmic city filth
striking against
his well-dressed body

hearses roll by, iron-clad wheels rattling,
urging city rats to scamper
past bluebottle flies
hovering over animal corpses
littering over city streets
like masses on an artery

a man walks through the city
as summer rots
locomotive steam pluming upward,
conjoining with polluted clouds,
soot and smoke
thickening a blockage from the sun

1886, late summer, early morning
a man steps off a train,
the clot breaks free, travels through
Chicago's body,
this dark-mustached swindler,
this charmer who pied the snakes
swallowed them whole,

emits musical poison from his throat
walks past death without blinking
thirty-five years old, five foot eight

blue eyes
hungering over
the sight of maggots
wondering how squirming larvae
would look
inside the body of the pretty woman
he had sat next to on the train.

Exploring the Monstrous Woman Archetype: Writing *Satan's Sweethearts*

Marge Simon

Mary Turzillo and I have several collaborations under our belts, such as our poetry collection *Sweet Poison*, which was a Bram Stoker award finalist. We decided that monstrous women, much like monstrous men, have been around since before recorded time, so when Mary mentioned the idea of poems based on the most contemptable women in history, I was all for it. We titled our collection *Satan's Sweethearts,* though it also could have also been something like *Monstrous Maidens*. Defining the archetype became the mission of our collection.

Our collection wasn't an easy one to write. By the time Mary and I finished, *Satan's Sweethearts* was a collection that well illustrated the monstrous woman with poems relating to despicable women, both past and present. The archetype is not a pretty creature; she wears many faces, comes in all races and colors, and hides behind numerous facades. Once we got into it, we realized that we had taken on a very difficult project. Ultimately, we needed someone to help put the archetype—or types, as it were, in perspective. To do this, we enlisted help from a brilliant writer/poet, David E. Cowen. He arranged our poems into sections with the following titles, each an incarnation of the elusive Monstrous Woman archetype:

- A Mother Only Satan Could Love–women *with no sense of motherly love*
- Sisters of Dreadful Mercy–women *who choose helpless victims*
- Sister Dread and Daughter Death–women who *kill for the sake of killing*
- The Last Wives' Club–*mercenary or manipulative women*
- Dames from the Deepest Circle of Hell–*psychotics, man haters, and sadists*

Some women were so bad that we had to step away and do something else before returning to finish the poem. We both had particular women in mind, (hers was Jodi Arias, and mine was Aileen Wuornos). For more examples, several sites online provide details of "The Most Evil Women in History." My preferred link: https://serialkillershop.com/blogs/true-crime/famous-female-serial-killers. There were even times when Mary admitted she was so horrified and depressed that she dodged the project. I took a break after writing some poems myself, such as with "Delphine LaLaurie's Upstairs Room." We both experienced headaches and mild depression. I turned to catching up on some illustration work.

In composing that particular poem, I researched obscure facts about LaLaurie, besides those of her dates of birth and death. I wanted the particulars, such as what the town firefighters found in a top floor room when a fire started in the kitchen of LaLaurie's house. I decided not to spotlight Delphine herself, but rather to let the evidence speak for itself. I opened that top story door, and there lay the bones of the poem:

Delphine LaLaurie's Upstairs Room

Her slaves they were,
with spiked collars
to remind them who was boss,
nails pulled out by the roots
two boys with mutilated privates,
none knew their names—

but there was pretty Kitta,
strung out on a bed,
intestines wrapped around her waist,
her brother, Sol, with
empty holes where once
his brown eyes shone,
guts nailed to the floor,

and her mother, partly skinned,
and amputated arms
"like a human caterpillar"
someone later notes,

and young Sam,
hair already white,
chained like the rest
to the wall,

lips sewn shut
over a mouthful of dung…

Most of the victims were still alive when rescued. They were taken to the town jail for want of a better place, and most of them died there. In this poem, I don't bring in Mrs. LaLaurie inflicting torture herself. I let the description of her victims do the talking as I describe the effects of her torture on each one. I also refrain from preachy or judgmental language.

Delphine represents women who enjoy acts of torture.

My first stanza begins without preamble. You might say it goes against the usual approach because there is no beautiful language, nor an abundance of adjectives or adverbs. Yet does it horrify? You bet.

Another woman of our times who was so terrible that the movie *Monster* was made about her was Florida's Aileen Wuornos. As I live in the state of the crimes, I followed reportage of her from the start, all the while wondering if I would ever chance to run into her sometime at a rest area on route to Tampa or Miami. In my piece "Born Mean," I use her final court statement as a preface to the poem:

> I killed those men, robbed them as cold as ice. And I'd do it again,
> too. There's no chance in keeping me alive or anything, because I'd
> kill again. I have hate crawling through my system…I am so sick of
> hearing this "she's crazy" stuff. I've been evaluated so many times.
> I'm competent, sane, and I'm trying to tell the truth. I'm one who
> seriously hates human life and would kill again. (Burkemann)

Touches like this work to lure in the reader, and you could even make up your own court statement or quote to fit your poem, depending on subject.

Born Mean

I was a bastard child,
born to a fourteen-year-old mother,
sired by a convicted felon;
I wasn't born crazy,
I was born mean.

Ladies you don't want to know
what your man is doing when he's on the road,
you think he's working hard to keep you happy?
get real --he's just another john.

Writing Poetry in the Dark

I put one of them down, and seven more,
between my legs with bullets in their lungs,
their balls, their fucking brains
yes, yes, yes and I'd do it again.

Florida isn't all you think,
it runs hot and it runs cold,
I got to get the hate out
it steams under my skin.

Truck stop lot lizards
got nothing on me—
I taught some of them,
screwed the rest …(extract)

The above is an example of using language to suit the style/voice of a poem. This poem shouts "I am Aileen. I grew up abused, motherless, unloved, and I'm one mean bitch." As a child, Aileen was raped by her grandfather and hated men. She was one tough cookie, and you don't need a lot of fancy adjectives to convey that.

Something else I like to ask myself when writing is what stands out in the poem? I wondered if a different voice or point of view would help enhance the character? In this case, I didn't think so. I was all for getting into her head, rather than elaborating on her motives or listing her crimes, but a different point of view was too impersonal; that's the law enforcement's job. For my purpose, first person makes this poem more memorable. With a character type like Aileen, I didn't have far to go to show her mindset and personality.

After all, her archetype kills for the sake of killing men.

Though some may disagree, I say most poems are transitory. That aside, put an effort into making your work memorable in some way, either by the point of view, the shape of it on the page, or by imagery, interior rhyme, or rhythms. In other words, compose to grab the reader's attention.

In my poem "The Goodbye Kiss," I give you a vision of revenge in the form of a vampire (or perhaps just a monstrous female vamp who kills her victims because she can't help it). The point of view is third person, one of the most tried and true for fantasy. Present tense is conducive to chilling touches that work well with the siren archetype.

162

The Goodbye Kiss

Behind her ears,
the scent of vanilla;
few men can resist,
if they are truly men.

The first stanza begins innocently enough. What can be purer than the scent of vanilla? In frontier days, vanilla was a young woman's perfume. You want to emphasize purity without using the word itself. Evil loves innocence, loves temptation, explodes eight cylinders with this female creature in full control all the way. We then move onto fully exploring the archetype and her response:

So he is just one more
lusting after her,
licking her skin,
touching certain private places
not allowed—
unaware of the cost,
the retribution for his sin.

She promises herself he'll be the last,
but it happens again and over,
each death unique as the one before.

Here is the enraged female, revolting against the mindless passions of a man who assumes he'll be her lover. He is not her first, we know this. She stands for revenge, for all young women at the mercy of their date's physical strength; thus the monstrous rises, plays its part. This action (though not described in detail) flows into a final stanza with a mystifying, blood-chilling finish.

Just one more, her lips fold softly
in a prayer to her dark goddess,
the one with the yellow eyes
who speaks in tongues.

I conjured our lady to right the injustices that young girls suffer when they're pawed at and poked by men, and it's not mutual. It's the *monstrous* feminine mystique in superpower action, but there is no mention of eating his face or tearing his organs out. If you read enough of my poems, you'll find I don't go in for gore or gross descriptions. Nor do I have some creepy monster rising from the shadows to eat the protagonist, who is usually their victim.

Why? I prefer subtlety. I love it. Why should I resort to tired descriptions of worms moving on corpses, or female zombies exacting vengeful evil by eating faces? It's a given that the horror genre takes on many forms and subjects. That said, my poems often purposely lack graphic descriptions, and I think for *Satan's Sweethearts*, that lack keeps my poems fresh. Mary's are all in keeping with this approach, too.

I also have a pet peeve about the word "monster" as a descriptor for a horrific evil person or thing if it stands alone in a poem. For example, "The monster was coming to get me." For effect, it's better to use "it" or "she," etc., because a monster, seen for the first time, should be something too terrible to describe with just one word. You want a poem to be memorable because it's good, not because of its trite descriptive language. When in doubt, give the facts and leave judgement to the reader.

Here are some more tips on the craft and development of your speculative poetry:

- Less is often more.
- Become familiar with the work of your successful peers. The Science Fiction and Fantasy Poetry Association (SFPA) and Horror Writers Association (HWA) are strongly recommended gateway organizations.
- Try different voices and perspectives (POV).
- Avoid judgmental language and prejudices. ("She was wicked, he was terrible, etc.)
- Research (first person accounts, news headlines, and history).
- Find your niche—remember, strive to discover fresh ways to use common words and descriptions. Try reading contemporary literary and genre (sf/h/f and speculative) magazines, both poetry and fiction. Your resources don't have to be strictly genre.

Freeing the Demon:
Writing Violence Into the Poem

Claire C. Holland

I can still see it in my mind. That hand.

I couldn't bear to look at everything, so I focused on the hand. Just the hand. The bruised, bulging shape of it, all purpled and swollen and sitting too near my face, which was nearly eye-level with the body in the casket. It looked like something dragged from the sea, and the pale, bloated skin looked shellacked with varnish, like the surface of a drum or the sail of a ship. Or a skin glove, tanned and stretched taut over the corpse's real hand.

The dead man was my neighbor, and I'd lived in the house next to him my entire life. He wasn't family, not technically, but my brother and I called him Uncle Chuck, and we called his wife Aunt Mary. They felt like family in that they were elderly and kind, and they were always around, tending to flowers or walking their small dog in the yard, ready with a wave and a moment to chat whenever I came home from school or a vacation. I took their presence for granted the way only an eight-year-old can, assuming they'd be there at least as long as I was. They were fixtures of the neighborhood, like the big yellow Labrador at the end of the block.

Until suddenly, they weren't.

As a kid, you only see events in relation to yourself. Uncle Chuck's death—the startling, brutal change in state from *here* to *not-here*—and the quick whisking away of Aunt Mary to a nursing home where she died soon after, felt not only incomprehensible to me, but deeply personal. His funeral was my first, and it was supposed to be a chance to say goodbye, but no one, I think, warned my parents that it would be open casket.

No one warned me.

I wasn't ready for it, and the unavoidable witnessing of his dead, wrong body felt like a kind of violence.

Childhood memory is turbulent, moored in time only by tragic and thrilling events strung together like buoys in the far-flung corners of the mind. So, it's either a terrible coincidence or just my brain linking memorable events together, but I remember watching the 1978 animated adaptation of Richard Adams' novel *Watership Down* not long after that funeral. Perhaps you know the book, but if not, a quick primer: It's about a warren of rabbits who are driven out of their natural habitat by developers and forced to find a new home. Along the way, they encounter foxes, traps and snares, cars, sinister societies of militant rabbits, farmers with shotguns, and more, all described in visceral detail.

The animated version, despite appearing to appeal to children at first glance, doesn't gloss over the violence in the novel one bit—and there are a thousand ways to die in *Watership Down*. Rabbits choke on poison gas or are snapped up in the jaws of a toothy predator. Rabbits are forced to rip others to shreds as a twisted form of punishment, while another painfully succumbs to the stranglehold of a wire snare.

My young brain wasn't ready for it.

Nightmares plagued me for weeks, fever dreams like nothing I'd experienced before: real rabbits clawing out their own eyes, gurgling and gasping on the blood suffocating their torn and ragged throats. Rabbits drowning in a sea of bubbling red and washing up on riverbanks next to disembodied hands and water-logged corpses, fur matted with gore. I couldn't get the images to stay out of my mind, but I pushed them as far back as I could. I vowed never to watch the movie again.

"Maybe you'll see it when you're older, and it won't be so bad," my dad, ever the professor, reasoned with me. "Or read the book."

I shook my head.

Only the passing of time made any real difference.

When art provokes—especially violent, morally ambiguous, or otherwise "uncomfortable" art—the question inevitably raised is: "Is it necessary?"

"It" being the violence. Or sometimes, the art itself, as if making it disappear could make the uncomfortable emotions vanish, too.

Society's relationship with violence is funny; it's all around us, casually, constantly, from sports and news to reality television. We delight in it as shallow entertainment but grow twitchy around art that engages with violence in nuanced and complex ways, anything that forces us to linger too close for too long and examine the core of the rotting thing. We're ill-at-ease with ambiguity—the bad teenagers must be punished and so forth, a tale as old as the MPAA—and violence is nothing if not a sea of gray tones.

We all know violence ourselves, though, have experienced it in infinite ways from the devastating to the nearly mundane. Rarely do these incidents feel insignificant. More often, they are a punch to the psyche, a yank on your tenuous world view. They are a beloved neighbor's dead hand or a blood-soaked bunny. They are jarring in their wrongness, and all our brains want is to set the world right again. Is it violent, then, to bring attention to the moments when most people would rather turn away? Is forcing a reader, even in the relatively gentle manner of a poem, to scrutinize something profoundly unsettling, violent? Perhaps jolting the reader out of the comfort of their personal experience is its own cruel act.

But is it necessary?

At some point in my gangly, anxiety-ridden tween years, I discovered that fear was cathartic and violence could be empowering. Not committing violent acts, but experiencing them through art.

I was a sheltered suburban kid—sheltered, but deeply curious. I sought out anything that felt dangerous and forbidden: books like *Flowers in the Attic* (a soapy series that follows the tragic and oft-incestuous lives of siblings forced to subsist in their grandmother's attic) and Larry Clark's fierce, carnal films about teenagers (*Kids* and *Bully* titillated and disgusted me at turns; I found their brew of sex and violence fascinating and endlessly rewatchable). Later, my friend and I would sneak down to my parents' basement for illicit viewings of *Mysterious Skin* and *Requiem for a Dream*, simultaneously shocked and in awe of the graphic scenes that unfolded in front of us. If violence can be boiled down to strength of emotion, then even our best intentions can be taken to ferocious ends. If anger can be violent, so can joy, or love. I discovered that a strong bout of emotion can be like a drug, driving people to do things they'd never normally consider doing.

It was a dreadfully exciting thought.

I devoured scenes and stories that pushed me to the emotional brink, even if they weren't my own, and they taught me things about myself I might never have learned otherwise. Every story I consumed felt like it was mining murky parts of myself, excising secret truths like glittering black gems. I held them close.

Eventually, my interest developed into an appetite for all things horror, but as my affinity grew, so did my self-consciousness. I wondered what assumptions people might make regarding my pull toward such grisly fare. What did it say about me, that these dark and thorny subjects spoke to me, stirred me, like nothing else had before? I was afraid to know, and so for years I kept those hungers largely to myself.

Be warned: such things have ways of getting out again.

In late 2016, two events of great significance occurred in my life: Donald Trump was elected president of the United States, and I began to write again—the second event being a result of my despair over the first.

Since graduating college, I'd wrestled extensively with the possibility of letting go of the idea of myself as a writer. I'd barely written anything in years, anyway, and it seemed quite possible that I might be a happier person if I put down my pen for good, made a clean break of it. Maybe if I wasn't always striving and searching for ideas, writing down half-finished lines in notebooks like they mattered, I would finally feel something like fulfillment. Maybe if I could stop beating myself up for the poems not written, I could be content. I could simply be done.

The 1981 horror film *Possession* is about the horrors of a crumbling marriage, but the movie focuses heavily on Anna's pain as the neglected wife in search of meaning. We're not privy to the specific events that led to the dissolution of the marriage, but signs hint at a growing distance and failure to communicate between Anna and her husband, Mark, a spy who spends extended amounts of time away from home. At one point, Anna prays to a crucifix in a church, seeking reassurance or comfort from God, but she receives nothing. Feeling empty, she makes her way back home.

Later, Anna describes to Mark a miscarriage she endured in the subway tunnel on her walk home that was not only physical, but also spiritual; fluids oozed from her orifices and her body convulsed in wild seizures, expelling all that she could no longer hold inside—her rage and resentment at her husband, her loss of faith. But it was the birth of something new in her, too: a new ethos, a different way of living. Something to believe in.

When last I saw this movie, I felt for Anna, but more to the point I felt *like* Anna—on the outside I was going through the motions, but on the inside, I was exhausted and raging and unable to communicate exactly why. The presidential election was the death knell, the straw that broke the camel's back in the end, but it had been building in me already for years, a discontentment. I felt on the edge of burnout all the time, stuck in a holding pattern between anxiety and anger, brought on by… I didn't know what. A job I didn't care about enough? Loneliness? Societal expectations that made me want to run away and live in the woods? Whatever it was, I couldn't articulate it to anyone, not even myself.

Seeing Anna roused something deep inside, something that resonated with a part of me I had yet to uncover but desperately wanted to explore. For the first time in ages, I found a poem pouring out of me.

Anna
Possession (1981)

A woman's body was made for this,
for birthing, for enduring

hours of pulsating pain, but no birth,
no ingress into this world should hurt

this much. A blade in her back,
it threatens to bubble up from inside,

to pour from her prone and twisting
body, everywhere, frothing

into cracks in the cement, heavy
like paint. And so she thrashes, smashes

her head against the tunnel walls
like a dervish, a devil woman demented

and godlike, with her too-many arms
waving, a container for grief and this other

thing she cannot name. A broken
discontent, willing itself to life.

This is what I have gathered from horror: If you don't release it, whatever *it* is, the lurid thing you keep hidden inside will claw its way up your throat and get out anyway.

This is a poem I wrote about one of the most violent things I can imagine, about the birth of something unspeakable made from your every suppressed and ugly thought rearing up at once. A monster of your mind's own making, obliterating everything you were before. It's violent, but maybe it's beautiful, too.

Writing Anna's poem dislodged something in me, and for months afterwards, I found myself again and again in the female characters of horror cinema. I found catharsis in surviving their harrowing experiences with them, as I always had, but now I was finding peace by borrowing their voices. By reinterpreting their violent experiences and the inconvenient emotions that came with them through the lens of poetry, I began to better understand my own anger and resentment, my own pull towards violence and other prickly things I didn't want to face. And I began to feel better.

I could say I wrote the poems to help other women, as a form of activism, perhaps. But the truth is that I wrote them because they were inside me, wrath and indignation clawing their way out, and they wouldn't, couldn't be stopped. I wrote them because there is something immediate and urgent about a poem that gets the point across like nothing else does. I wrote because it feels like the only way I can ever make other people understand anything, and I want to feel less alone on this planet. I wrote because it's the next best thing to committing murder.

I don't know if humans are violent by nature, but I know that we are all capable of violence, that we are all actually brimming with unpredictable impulses. So, what do we writers do with those impulses? We write, of course, and we write what *needs* to be written. By putting it down on the page—your unspeakable, unacceptable violence, whatever thrives in the honest, gory center of you—maybe we enact a bit of violence on our readers, too, but I believe that it is necessary. When we dig deep to reveal something true and then force others to see it, too, it can feel violent. But it's the violence of recognition, and by sharing it, we shift the power. We let go of shame.

Because violence rarely feels inconsequential in real life, I believe that violence in art should not feel inconsequential either. Uncomfortable, yes. Aggressive, even. Make your writing confrontational as hell. Make it exhilarating and unnerving. Make it bracing. Make it a wakeup call. But if nothing else, do one vital thing: make it necessary. I don't mean that you should censor yourself until you feel the violence in your poem has reached some socially acceptable threshold—to attempt that is to attempt the impossible, which is to try to please everyone. No, the slippery slope I worry about is self-censoring to avoid discomfort, to deny our most real and human parts because we're afraid of what will happen when we don't.

Violence is human. To repress things and try to pretend they don't exist, to oppress and deny the complete spectrum of our emotions in all their glorious potency—that, to me, is unnecessary violence. It's toxic and it leads to terrible art. Letting emotions fester and rot like so much garbage can only create something more poisonous and volatile, eager to will its own way to life.

I revisited *Watership Down* many years later, as an adult, and it was so much *less* than I remembered. I'd let nightmarish thoughts haunt my dreams for months, even years, and suddenly, so easily, I was able to let go of them completely. I haven't had a similar experience regarding the funeral, and that hand still looms large and loathsome in my memory. Maybe this will help. Maybe I still need to write a poem about it.

Writing is alchemy. You take scary, magical things like emotions—all your pain and anger, your joy and lust, everything you're afraid of—and you let them churn around inside the brilliant galaxy of your body and brain until they can't be contained anymore. Then you make something. Maybe you make art. Maybe it's violent art.

Whatever it is, make the thing that sets you free.

Dancing in the Design:
Creating Blackout Poetry

Jessica McHugh

I feel awkward breaking down my writing process for others. Even as I enter my thirteenth year of being a professional horror author with two dozen published books, five years of teaching creative writing workshops, and a Bram Stoker-nominated blackout poetry collection, I have trouble articulating the hows and whys behind my art. Perhaps because I don't always understand them myself.

But that's not a problem when it comes to blackout poetry, since the hows and whys frequently change. I also don't start a piece focusing on the rules of the craft, or even the results. Blackout poetry is a roller coaster built upon the love of words, their rhythms, shapes, and colors, and the excitement of finding the correct configuration of controlled chaos to touch someone's soul. Or turn their stomach. It encourages the poet to live in the moment, thirsty for adventure, like a diver exploring a new reef, or a baby witch building her first spell.

That's how I feel as I begin: daring and magical.

Free, too.

But despite my belief that blackout poetry doesn't abide by traditional rules, I've learned a few tricks for newcomers to keep in mind as they hunt for the hidden poem in their favorite books.

Difficult as it can be, I find it's best to dissociate my mind from the intent of the original prose, viewing it as a sea of random words instead. Some of these words will shine like buoys between the waves—I take note of them as I scan the page—but finding my anchor word (or words) is my most important goal. It will serve as the subject—or a metaphor for the subject—of my poem. In the case of the attached piece, "Hungry" from my collection *Strange Nests*, I anchored the flow of my poem to "earth" and "throat." After scanning the surrounding prose, it became the opener, "You're the earth in my throat," thereby establishing the theme for the rest of the poem.

From that point on, it's an artistic word search. Because of this, metaphor and simile work extremely well. Phrases like "I am..." or "Love is...," or the contracted "You are..." in "Hungry," might seem like cliché ways to start a piece but considering the linguistic wilderness that comprises the rest of the page, leading the reader from simplicity into a beautiful or horrific metaphor can be a shockingly deep and transformative journey.

Another option is approaching it like flash fiction. Blackout poetry, like flash, is a test in brevity—with added language and space constraints. Having fewer words available to manipulate makes word economy vital. It's imperative to choose words and phrases that evoke emotion quickly, while being aware of how their value changes when rearranged or with their tenses altered. The more it's practiced, the more second-nature it becomes. This talent also aids in long-form writing, so even if blackout and flash aren't your favorite art forms, experimenting with both can be beneficial elsewhere.

While this medium has many names—blackout, erasure, redacted— found poetry feels most accurate for pre-colored works-in-progress. While I'm writing the poem, I'm a treasure hunter, I'm a builder, I'm a sculptor, I'm a scavenger, I'm a sorceress, I'm a mother trying to wrangle word-children playing hide-and-go-seek in department store clothing racks. I'm also a risk-taker. With every swoop of the pencil, every swipe of the eraser, the page remembers. Depending on the book's age, I might only get one chance to erase something, lest I strip the ink out of the paper. This terror will, of course, be experienced again once the coloring process begins, but I like a little time to sit with my poem before I dive into those waters.

There's a palpable feeling of triumph once I've found/written a poem. It's so strong, in fact, that I have over fifty creations that haven't moved beyond this stage. But they don't torture me the way incomplete projects in other mediums do. In fact, having poems in this stage proved extremely helpful while I was grieving the loss of my brother earlier this year. I couldn't write prose or poetry in that state, but I could color. I could put all of my anger and sorrow into the design of pieces I'd written months, even years, prior.

It was then that I realized blackout poetry doesn't only require an anchor. For me, it can also *be* an anchor. Coloring those pieces kept me grounded in the weeks following Eric's death and eventually led me back to creating new pieces: notably horror poems like "Hungry," which I found in the Frances

Hodgson Burnett classic, *The Secret Garden*, and is now one of my favorite pieces in *Strange Nests*.

There's a lot of magic in blackout poetry. I often feel like Merricat from Shirley Jackson's *We Have Always Lived in the Castle* with her words of power and protection. The phrases that leap out when I scan a fresh page feel important, even fated, as if the story from which I'd sworn to divorce myself were giving my soul glimpses of its most distilled and potent messages.

This is more common when creating multiple pieces from the same book, as I do for collections and commissions. As much as you disassociate from the original material, each word is still a part of a greater narrative. Discovering those peekaboo themes in *The Secret Garden* is the reason I latched on so hard two weeks after my brother died. After finding a few poems, I knew I had to create a collection that told a story about grief, possession, and transformation: all of which appear thematically in *The Secret Garden*. It provided the perfect canvas for horror poetry and art. As it turns out, a lot of books do, no matter the genre.

Horror dwells comfortably in blackout poetry because it's as quick and deep as a shiv, but if the wound is well-made, the reader will be too busy dancing in blood puddles to notice you're dragging the blade.

And I love dancing with them.

Using intriguing and unexpected shapes and linework, I draw in the reader's focus and make their eyes cavort across the page while I take their minds on a darker journey. With bold colors highlighting evocative words, grotesque illustration or papercraft in the margins, or other tools like peeling off superfluous ink with tape, a thoughtful design works in tandem with the writing to conjure feelings of anxiety, claustrophobia, or abyssal emptiness.

I don't usually ponder the visual sense of the piece too deeply until I'm happy with what I've written, but it helps to be mindful of the path I'm creating as I build a poem. It doesn't have to start at the top or flow in traditional directions—you can even borrow letters to build words, like I did with "you're" and "new" in the attached piece—but a certain legibility should be maintained or at least controlled through the design. Because "Hungry" is a longer piece with several separate thoughts closely clustered, I felt the addition of a connecting line would help steer the reader, while the pronounced dots on either end of those lines suggest a starting and ending point to prevent the eye from running it all together. But with the papercraft teeth on the top and bottom, the lines also mimic intestines, which represents the poem's vibe perfectly.

The blackout/coloring process is an opportunity to show off the poem's personality. Sometimes a simple approach best serves the piece—minimal colors, clean strikethroughs, words crisply circled or outlined—and sometimes the poem demands to be heard in bombastic shades of neon, in glitter and gore. Sometimes I lean into typical hues to convey certain emotions, and other times I seek out new and intriguing ways to convey universal themes. Maybe love isn't red or pink; maybe it's dark brown with the shimmer of moisture, like the deep, fertile earth where we all started. Maybe death isn't black, but yellow, like a bruise that never quite heals.

Blackout poetry actively encourages experimentation. My designs were fairly simplistic when I started, relying mostly on color to enhance the poem. But the more I made, the more variation I craved, the more techniques I wanted to try, and the more crafty art supplies I wanted to collect. I did some illustration in the beginning, but I didn't think I had much talent in that area, so I did papercraft a lot more. I didn't have much experience with papercraft at the time either, but it felt like a safer challenge than drawing directly on the page.

Plus, I really enjoy making puppy dogs and scary teeth and glittery multicolored dragon scales.

Papercraft led to collage work, which I played around with while working with the beautiful illustrations of famed muralist Graham Rust in my copy of *The Secret Garden*. But while collaging someone else's artwork is fine for personal use, it's not legal to publish, and Mr. Rust, kind and sympathetic though he was in our correspondence, couldn't grant me publication rights. But necessity is the mother of invention, and with my grief and hope already bound to *The Secret Garden*, I needed to rethink my strategy, especially since I'd already finished seven pieces. Painful as it was deconstructing those poems, it forced me to look my fear of illustration in the eye and conquer it. Much like finding words, the more I drew, the more I worked to expose their personalities through shape and color, the better I got. Once I was able to quell that anxiety, I felt like there was nothing I couldn't do. I made bigger pieces, ones with elements that spin and even move around the page. With each blackout poem, I have an opportunity to create something that's truly unique, and once I chose to let go of my fear of making mistakes, I had real artistic freedom.

You can paint over it, slice into it, use the words in a collage, sew the words into formation, make something three-dimensional, and yes, you will make mistakes, but there's almost always a way to either disguise or incorporate those errors into the piece. And you'd be surprised at how resilient some books are when it comes to using different inks and paints. When I was commissioned to make horror poetry from the Bible, I was worried the paper itself would be limiting. But I was way off. While it did crease and tear easily, it took color and sparkle better than any other book I've worked with. It was such a fun discovery in an art form full of fun discoveries.

These a-ha moments are some of the best parts of creating art. Even writing this essay—something that admittedly gave me discomfort—has bestowed gifts of discovery along the way. I actually understand my hows and whys better now, and as I have with many lessons that blackout poetry has taught me, I'll take that newfound understanding into other mediums.

As a writer who plays in a lot of sandboxes, there's another big element of the writing process that unnerves me and that's thinking up the perfect title. If I haven't thought of one by the time everything else is said and done, I agonize over it. However, much like speaking about my process, I don't have that problem with blackout poetry. Like the poem itself, I also find my title in the sea of words—the same words that jumped out at me while writing, actually…except, on the other side of the page. I hold it up to the light to see which words appear outlined and then create a title from those options. It's proven effective due to the proximity of the poem as there's a good chance whatever was happening in the original prose on one side is still occurring on the other. The title "Hungry," for example, was waiting on the other side of "You," the first word of the poem, and it perfectly embodies the mood. It feels like another bit of magic when the title fits into place like that: the last piece of the puzzle.

I'm hoping it'll happen again as I attempt to title this essay. With my mind a whirling mess of possibilities pulling me this way and that, I once again look to blackout poetry to anchor me. And, as I found on the inverse of the blackout poem I made from the first two pages of this essay, I hope to always keep "dancing in the design."

"Where do you play?" he asked next.

"Everywhere," gasped Mary. "Martha's mother sent me a skipping-rope. I skip and run—and I look about to see if things are beginning to stick up out of the earth. I don't do any harm."

"Don't look so frightened," he said in a worried voice. "You could not do any harm, a child like you! You may do what you like."

Mary put her hand up to her throat because she was afraid he might see the excited lump which she felt jump into it. She came a step nearer to him.

"May I?" she said tremulously.

Her anxious little face seemed to worry him more than ever.

"Don't look so frightened," he exclaimed. "Of course you may. I am your guardian, though I am a poor one for any child. I cannot give you time or attention. I am too ill, and wretched and distracted; but I wish you to be happy and comfortable. I don't know anything about children, but Mrs Medlock is to see that you have all you need. I sent for you today because Mrs Sowerby said I ought to see you. Her daughter had talked about you. She thought you needed fresh air and freedom and running about."

"She knows all about children," Mary said again in spite of herself.

"She ought to," said Mr Craven. "I thought her rather bold to stop me on the moor, but she said Mrs Craven had been kind to her." It seemed hard for him to speak his dead wife's name. "She is a respectable woman. Now I have seen you I think she said sensible things. Play out of doors as much as you like. It's a big place, and you may go where you like and amuse yourself as you like. Is there anything you want?" As if a sudden thought had struck him. "Do you want toys, books, dolls?"

"Might I," quavered Mary, "might I have a bit of earth?"

In her eagerness she did not realize how queer the words would sound and that they were not the ones she had meant to say. Mr Craven looked quite startled.

"Earth!" he repeated. "What do you mean?"

"To plant seeds in—to make things grow—to see them come alive," Mary faltered.

He gazed at her a moment and then passed his hand quickly over his eyes.

"Do you—care about gardens so much?" he said slowly.

"I didn't know about them in India," said Mary. "I was always ill and

Writing the Wound

Donna Lynch

When I put together my first poetry collection in the late '90s, I was almost proud to say that my writing was not the catharsis that so many writers before me had claimed when talking about their own work. Looking back, I don't know why I said that. Maybe I felt it made me seem stronger, like I had forged my way through the dark experiences and emotions I wrote about and somehow come out hardened and ready to tell my stories from a safe distance, someplace far away from the feelings. Thinking this was a desirable trait surely came from a toxic mindset, one that probably began with being told again and again that I was much too sensitive, too easily injured, and that being tough—whatever that meant—was the only way to earn respect. It would be years before I learned the extent of the damage this caused, and it's safe to say that my work came from an unintentionally disingenuous place up until my performative shell finally cracked in the late 2000s.

That crack became an irreparable breach in the wake of a profound loss, and it led to the first accurate mental health diagnosis I'd received in years. What we'd formally acknowledged as depression was just one side of my Bipolar II and Emotionally Unstable Personality Disordered life. We'd written off the other manic side as severe anxiety, impulsivity, selfishness, and poor choices. Even with medication and regular therapy, I struggled with empathy and the treacherous ability to compartmentalize, but something I could never shake was the idea that no one *chooses* to set their life on fire; people don't opt to live in a fluctuating state of emptiness and chaos. No one wants that. There's not a single benefit to it.

When I see someone going off the rails, I don't think *what a train wreck*. I think *that person is sick, and I wish someone could help them see it*. I know what it feels like to have people think you're being a terrible person, when really, you are stuck in self-destruct mode and don't recognize it or have the slightest idea how to stop it. When you are wired this way, and have a creative mind on top of that, it's remarkable the complex stories you can weave to keep yourself afloat. But sooner or later, those words break down to pulp in the water and you sink.

This essay isn't about my personal journey, but I've shared the above because it was the impetus for a huge shift in my writing and leads us to the topic-at-hand: writing the wound.

When my poetry got honest—when **I** got honest—it got better. The more it hurt to write, the more impact it had. And the more I opened up, the stronger I became. Real strength. Healthy strength. Not *I'm-terrified-people-will-think-I'm-weak-so-I-better-pretend-otherwise* strength. I also learned that there needs to be a balance. You can bleed onto the page, but you need to be able to clot when it's time. The solution to damage isn't more damage.

It's hard, but as I do the work to remain stable, it gets easier. We are so scared of hurting, even just being uncomfortable, and rightfully so. It sucks. But to paraphrase one of my favorite musicians and writers, Nick Cave— feeling pain is the deal you make in order to experience love. In my piece "All the Things They Never Tell You" I address this with the line, "One day you will lose everything you love," which refers not to a matter of fault, but an absolute guarantee. It's a painful, uncomfortable thought, and the act of writing it down hurt, because—having committed to writing honestly—it was the first time I knew I believed it, and I hated every keystroke.

I felt that same anger and upset when I wrote more personal pieces, not those about the existential crisis that we all experience at some point, but those about my own darkness. But this time, a new emotion crept in— shame. I saw myself and the things I'd done, or had been done to me, in *real* words. My words. There are still many words I haven't written, but these things take time.

Writing honestly in horror means walking straight into those dark woods and abandoned houses, the graveyards and the much-too-idyllic neighborhoods and recording every ugly, bizarre thing found there. Sometimes you find fear and dread, and sometimes you find all manner of entities and haunted relics, possession and even psychosis. But sometimes you find nothing. Imagine looking into a mirror and not only *not* seeing your reflection but realizing there's no glass. You thought there was glass. Surely, there *must* have been glass. There was no witch, no monster, no cursed box. It was just you.

There's nothing wrong with metaphors and allegories, nothing wrong at all with haunted stories and folk tales and modern myths. They are among my favorite elements of storytelling, but when it comes to addressing our illnesses and traumas, they can act as a protective shell.

So, do you want to break it apart and find out what's inside?

How do you find the words to describe that feeling? When you've written all the murder and gore and rage, all the ghosts, the symbolic acts and metaphors of your trauma, what's left? When you've dug into the wound, down through the layers of skin and scar tissue, through the muscle and fat, and hit bone, what do you say? Is that all there is?

Horror works for the same reason any genre works: it's relatable.

Stories in all other genres speak to us, and they appease our desires. Some make us feel understood. Some confirm that we aren't alone in our fantasies.

Horror often gets thrown under the bus, stripped of its profound impact on society and accused of serving no purpose other than to make people feel terrible. But none of that is true. Horror can make us feel seen. It feeds into our fears and nightmares, yes, but it bleeds into our dreams. In the Clive Barker film *Nightbreed* (adapted from his book *Cabal*), one of the Breed, Rachel, says, "To be able to fly, to be smoke, or a wolf? To know the night and live in it forever? That's not so bad. You call us 'monsters,' but when you dream, you dream of flying, and changing, and living without death." Fear is not something we can eliminate by closing our eyes; it's not something we should eliminate at all. We can run, but it will catch us. Always. Horror is a tool that affords us a sense of control over the inevitable. If we just let ourselves be afraid, maybe we can stop running so hard.

As storytellers, we get to wield that sense of control with our words, and we can create whatever specs we choose, and if we make it wide enough and deep enough, the more area it covers and the more inclusive it becomes. And with that inclusion, we find our common ground and our relatable fears. Being wounded, and the *fear of* being wounded, is some of the most common ground we share.

If you write that, you *will* be seen and understood.

Going back to achieving balance—the clotting, as it were—the goal in writing this kind of brutally honest pain and fear—the kind that comes from shining the light into yourself, rather than into the dark woods or a haunted house—is not to injure, but to acknowledge.

Of course, I want to evoke intense emotion. I also want to keep you reading. But more than that, I want to leave you with something you can use, whether it be a method of voyeuristic entertainment, a tool for introspection, that sense of feeling less alone in your pain, or maybe all of the above. But if I attempt to gut you without a vein of honesty and compassion, I will fail to give you any of those things. So there needs to be an agreement proposed between writer and reader: I'll show you my wounds and hopefully, it will entice you or compel you to look at yours. If it does, we've made a connection. We've found common ground, established empathy, and we don't have to be afraid of bleeding out.

Poetry isn't a free-for-all, there are rules—but my favorite thing about the medium is the variety of structure a writer can choose from. Try to intertwine it with the desired atmosphere: the child-like eeriness of a rhyme scheme or use the same style to create a juxtaposition—a brutal story told like a sweet song. We're painting a graphic picture with the broad strokes of free form, conveying space and silence with word formatting, or conversely, creating confusion or claustrophobia, all the while ensuring that the reader has an immersive experience through our words and their placement.

When you read something horrific, have you ever taken notice of where you feel it in your body?

A dear friend, who is a psychologist, talked with me about this: paying attention to where you feel your thoughts. When you are afraid, do you feel your throat or chest tighten? Do you feel a fluttering in your stomach? Have you ever been so afraid that you felt a heat rising between your legs or in your bladder like a flush you can't control? What about a full body shudder?

I write body horror and have a fascination with biology and anatomical anomalies, so I'm far from squeamish, but I can vividly remember so many times I was reading something that truly made me nauseated, cold sweats and all. Endeavor to make your reader not just think the thoughts, but to feel it somewhere else inside of them as they take in the words. The best way to do this is to write the things that make you, yourself, feel that way.

When we tell our stories, our tales of pain and struggle and fear, it's normal to want to address every detail. Maybe if we set the scene perfectly and give ALL THE CONTEXT, it will be easier for people to relate. And that's perfectly fine. It's called venting. But one of the beautiful elements of poetry is the culling of the words. Of course, we can fill the page as much as we want—there are so many forms and traditions, depending on our needs—but I have always loved the challenge of getting inside the reader's mind with a few choice phrases—like casting a simple spell that flings open a door. Songwriters do it all the time, and there's no reason you can't use a song format as an infrastructure for your poem. Leave out the minutiae—the parts that sound like you're making a police report—and focus on the words that set the scene and then paint the picture for your verses. Then, for your chorus, create the *hook* from what it made you feel. It works in poetry just as it works in songwriting.

With every line, consider what it contributed to the piece. If the answer is "not much," take it out and substitute it with something that *sings* or fill the space with silence.

This culling goes a long way when trying to write an impactful piece that others will let into their hearts. It's what makes it poetry, and what makes it different from journaling or narrating.

My personal goal these days with horror poetry has been not to cause the wounds or even open them, but to find a place to nestle within the ones that are already there, holding space as I use them to create and connect. Yes, we will be hurt in our lives. We will be afraid of so many things. We will suffer loss. This is guaranteed. My writing career in horror has, in part, been my outlet to cope with the immutable and inevitable—all that has happened and all that is to come. We don't have to share the same goals, but the deeper you dig, you may find that yours are similar. You don't always have to set out to fabricate fear.

Instead, be the mirror in which people see their pain. Be the light that shines upon atrocity, revealing it.

Tell the stories of the wounded with eloquence or brutality—whatever it takes to make us feel—but above all else, tell the stories with honesty.

Show us the wounds.

All the Things They Never Tell You

When Witches get trapped in hallway mirrors
and those mirrors break
It just makes more witches

The Devil doesn't possess children
He just takes the blame
So no one has to face the fact that
some children are broken for no reason

Angels walk among us
but they are not love, they are not here to help
Not a single one

When people die
They feel like cold, heavy meat
Even the ones you love

No one will ever notice you
as much as those who wish to see you suffer
those who wish to see you fail
And those people will notice *everything*
Every *single* thing you do
is a desperate attempt to evade fear
deep down inside
Your body will betray you
Your brain will betray you worse
but will lie and tell you otherwise

And one day you will lose everything you love
which is the most terrifying
Of all the things they never tell you.

Endnotes

"To Sing Dark Songs" by Tim Waggoner
- Waggoner, Tim. *Writing in the Dark.* Dog Star Books, 2020.
- Waggoner, Tim. *Writing in the Dark: The Workbook.* Guide Dog Books, 2022.

"Dislocating the World" by F.J. Bergmann
- Armitage, Simon. "Dämmerung." *Poets.org*, 2014.
- Bergman, F.J. "Avocation." *Asimov's SF,* 2018.
- Bergman, F.J. "*A Catalog of the Furter Suns.* Gold Line Press, 2017.
- Bergmann, F.J. "Fame." *Weird Tales 350*, 2009.
- Bergman, F.J. "Further." *The Lovecraft eZine*, 2016.
- Bergmann, F.J. "Maculation." *Spectral Realms, No. 10*, Hippocampus Press, 2019.
- Bergman, F.J. "Night Shift." *The Pedestal Magazine*, 2012.
- Bergmann, F.J. *Out of the Black Forest.* Centennial Press, 2012.
- Bergman, F.J. "A Woman of a Certain Age." *Apex Magazine.* 2011.
- Collins, Billy. *180 More: Extraordinary Poems for Every Day.* Random House, 2005.
- Mathys, Ted. "Let Muddy Water Sit and It Grows Clear." *Poets.org,* 2015.
- Duhamel, Denise and Sandy McIntosh. *237 More Reasons to Have Sex.* Lulu.com, 2011.

"Writing Speculative Poetry in Experimental Forms" by Linda D. Addison
- Addison, Linda D. "D2D Candy Corn." *Southwest Review*, Vol 106.3, 2021,
- Addison, Linda D., and Stephen M. Wilson. *Dark Duet.* Necon Modern Horror, CreateSpace Independent Publishing, 2013.
- Collings, Michael R. *The Arts and Craft of Poetry: Twenty Exercises Toward Mastery.* Wildside Press, 2014.
- Hayes, Terrance. "The Golden Shovel." *Lighthead: Poems.* Penguin Books, 2010.
- Goldberg, Natalie. *Writing Down the Bones: Freeing the Writer Within.* Shambhala, 2016.
- Kahn, Peter, Ravi Shankar, and Patricia Smith. *The Golden Shovel Anthology: New Poems Honors Gwendolyn Brooks*. The University of Arkansas Press, 2019.

"The Art of Speculative Haiku" by Christina Sng

- Sng, Christina. "all this rain." *Star*Line 44.1*, 2021.
- Sng, Christina. "android apocalypse." *Star*Line 43.3*, 2020.
- Sng, Christina. "an eternal divide." *Astronomers Without Borders Global Astronomy Month AstroPoetry Contest*, 2018.
- Sng, Christina "just wanting." *Scifaikuest*, 2016.
- Sng, Christina. "a leaf on a journey." *Haiku University's Haiku Column*. Daily Best, 2021.
- Sng, Christina. "Little Red in Haiku." *Star*Line 40.4*, 2017.
- Sng, Christina. "mesmerized by sunlight." *Scifaikuest*, 2019.
- Sng, Christina. "multiverse theory this feeling of déjà vu." *Sonic Boom 9*, 2017.
- Sng, Christina. "a paper plane." *Scifaikuest*, 2019.
- Sng, Christina. "seeing stars." *Scifaikuest*, 2019.
- Sng, Christina. "snowy plans." *Scifaikuest*, 2020.
- Sng, Christina. "within sight." *Scifaikuest*, 2019.
- Sng, Christina. "a world." *Star*Line 39.4*, 2016.

"A Slippery World: Writing Poetry About Gender & Sexuality" by Lucy A. Snyder

- Plath, Sylvia. "Mad Girl's Love Song." *Mademoiselle*, 1953.
- Snyder, Lucy A. "Cougar." *Orchid Carousals*. Creative Guy Publishing, 2013.

"Do Not Fear Poetry Collaboration" by Jim and Janice Leach

- Esaias, Timons. "Horror 01." *Edgar: Digested Verse #3*, Summer 1999.
- Heen, Shelia, and Douglas Stone. *Thanks for the Feedback: The Science and Art of Receiving Feedback Well*. Penguin Books, 2015.
- Leach, Janice and James Frederick Leach. *'Til Death: Marriage Poems*. Raw Dog Screaming Press, 2017.

"Here Are the Stairs to the Dark Cellar; Yes, You Must Go There: POV in Dark Poetry" by Timons Esaias

- Simon, Marge. "April Moon." *Bete Noire*, 2017.
- Tantlinger, Sara. "Dark Appetites." *The Devil's Dreamland: Poetry Inspired by H. H. Holmes*. StrangeHouse Books, 2018.
- Turzillo, Mary. "Tatiana." *Lovers & Killers*. Dark Regions Press, 2012.

"World-Building...in a *Poem*?" by Albert Wendland

- Wendland, Albert. *Temporary Planets for Transitory Days: Poems of Mykol Ranglen*. Raw Dog Screaming Press, 2020.

"Putting the Science in Science Fiction Poetry" by Jeannine Hall Gailey
- Gailey, Jeannine Hall. "Cesium Burns Blue" and "Robot Scientist's Daughter: Medical Wonder." *The Robot Scientist's Daughter*. Mayapple Books, 2015.
- Gailey, Jeannine Hall. "Chaos Theory." *Becoming the Villainess*. Steel Toe Books, 2006.
- Gailey, Jeannine Hall. "The Last Love Poem." *Field Guide to the End of the World*. Moon City Press, 2016
- Smith, Tracy K. *Life on Mars*: *Poems*. Graywolf Press, 2011.

"Like Fright on Lice: Humor and Horror Poetry" by Michael Arnzen
- Arnzen, Michael. *The Gorelets Omnibus*. Raw Dog Screaming Press, 2012.
- Carroll, Lewis. "Jabberwocky." *The Random House Book of Poetry for Children*. 1983.
- Hamby, Barbara, and David Kirby. *Seriously Funny: Poems about Love, Death, Religion, Art, Politics, Sex, and Everything Else*. University of Georgia Press, 2010.
- Lawson, Jenny. *Furiously Happy: A Funny Book About Horrible Things*. Flatiron Books, 2017.
- Williams, William Carlos. "The Red Wheelbarrow." *The Collected Poems of William Carlos Williams, Volume 1, 1909-1939*, edited by Christopher MacGowan, 1938.

"Dark Poetry and War" by Alessandro Manzetti
- Manzetti, Alessandro, and Marge Simon. *War: Dark Poems*. Crystal Lake Publishing, 2018.

"This Is Not A Poem" by Cynthia Pelayo
- Acevedo, Elizabeth. "An Open Letter to the Protestors Outside the Planned Parenthood Near My Job." *Women of Resistance: Poems for a New Feminism*. OR Books, 2018.
- Angelou, Maya. "Still I Rise." *And Still I Rise: A Book of Poems*. Random House, 1978.
- Browne, Mahogany L. "For Black and Brown Girls Gone Missing." *VIBE Magazine*, 4 April 2017, https://www.youtube.com/

watch?v=8vAHS0Voo4I. Accessed 9 June 2022.
- Ginsberg, Allen. "Howl." *Howl and Other Poems*. City Lights Books, 1956.
- Gorman, Amanda. "The Hill We Climb." *The Hill We Climb: An Inaugural Poem for the Country.* Viking Books, 2021.
- Hughes, Langston. "Harlem." *Montage of a Dream Deferred*. Holt, 1951.
- Pelayo, Cynthia. *Into the Forest and All the Way Through*. Burial Day Books, 2020.
- "Global Reflections Within Our Fear-Lit Ink: A Study on Tradition and Community in the Poem" by Bryan Thao Worra

Erdrich, Louise, "Windigo," *Jacklight*, Holt, New York, NY, 1984.
- Kaignavongsa, Xay, "The Frog Who Eats The Moon," *Legends of the Lao*, Allied Printers, Saskatchewan, CA. 1993. p. 7.
- Nash, Ogden, "The Wendigo." *Custard the Dragon and the Wendigo*, F. Warne, Lodon, 1977.
- Reed, Ishmael, "Beware: Do Not Read This Poem," *Catechism of d Neoamerican Hoodoo Church*. (Heritage Series, Volume 11), Paul Breman, London, 1970.
- "A Size-Up of President Nixon: Interview with Mike Mansfield, Senate Democratic Leader". *U.S. News & World Report.* December 6, 1971. p. 61.
- Worra, Bryan Thao. *Demonstra: A Poetry Collection*. Innsmouth Free Press, 2013.

"Of Poison Doors and Uncarved Stones: Myth as A Means to Mystery & Ecstasy in Speculative Poetry" by Saba Syed Razvi, PhD
- Razvi, Saba Syed. "A Note on the Setting of the Type." In the Crocodile Gardens, Agape Editions, 2016, page 92.

"Into the Dark Woods: Fairy Tale Poetry" by Carina Bissett
- Apuleius. *The Golden Ass: The Transformation of Lucius*. Translated by Robert Graves. Farrar, Straus and Giroux, 2009.
- Asbjørnsen, Peter Christen and Jørgen Moe. *East of the Sun and West of the Moon: Old Tales From the North*. Project Gutenberg, 2010, https://www.gutenberg.org/ebooks/30973. Accessed 13 June 2022.
- Barbot de Villenueve, Gabrielle-Suzanne. *Beauty and the Beast*. Pook Press, https://www.pookpress.co.uk/beaumont-beauty-beast/. Accessed on 9 June 2022.

- Basile, Giambattista. *The Tale of Tales*. Penguin Classics, 2016.
- Bissett, Carina. "Seven Swans." *Journal of Mythic Arts*, 2000.
- Child, Francis James. *The English and Scottish Popular Ballads Vol. 1-5*. Forgotten Books, 2007.
- Cox, Marian Roalfe. *Cinderella: Three Hundred and Forty-Five Variants of Cinderella*. Alpha Edition, 2020.
- Duffy, Carol Ann. *The World's Wife: Poems*. Farrar, Straus and Giroux, 2001.
- Gaiman, Neil. "Instructions." *Journal of Mythic Arts*, 2000.
- Gill, Nikita. *Fierce Fairytales: Poems and Stories to Stir Your Soul*. Hachette Books, 2018.
- Graça da Silva, Sara, and Jamshid J. Tehrani. "Comparative phylogenetic analyses uncover the ancient roots of Indo-European folktales." *Royal Society Open Science*, vol. 3, no. 1, 1 Jan. 2016, https://royalsocietypublishing.org/doi/10.1098/rsos.150645. Accessed 13 June 2022.
- Goss, Theodora. *Snow White Learns Witchcraft: Stories and Poems*. Mythic Delirium Books, 2019.
- Grimm, Jacob and Wilhelm Grimm. *The Original Folk and Fairy Tales of the Brothers Grimm*. Edited and translated by Jack Zipes, Princeton University Press, 2016.
- Lang, Andrew. *The Blue Fairy Book*. Project Gutenberg, 2005, https://www.gutenberg.org/ebooks/503. Accessed 13 June 2022.
- Lang, Andrew. *The Lilac Fairy Book*. Project Gutenberg, 2002, https://www.gutenberg.org/ebooks/3454. Accessed 13 June 2022.
- Langrish, Katherine. *Seven Miles of Steel Thistles: Reflections on Fairy Tales*. Independently published, 2016.
- Mark, Sabrina Orah. "The Evil Stepmother." *The Paris Review*, 2019.
- Perrault, Charles. "Cendrillon, ou La Petite Pantoufle de Verre." *Pook Press*, https://www.pookpress.co.uk/cendrillon-french-cinderella-perrault/. Accessed on 9 June 2022.
- Sexton, Anne. *Transformations*. Ecco, 2001.
- Sng, Christina. *A Collection of Dreamscapes*. Raw Dog Screaming Press, 2020.
- Sng, Christina. *A Collection of Nightmares*. Raw Dog Screaming Press, 2017.
- Warner, Marina. *Once Upon a Time. A Short History of Fairy Tale*. Oxford University Press, 2016.

"Dreams as Poetry: Translating Dreams into Verse" by Joanna C. Valente
- Doolittle, Hilda. "Eurydice." *Poetry Foundation*, 1982.

- Rossetti, Christina. "Goblin Market." *Poetry Foundation,* 1862.
- Valente, Joanna. *Marys of the Sea. Second Expanded ed.*, The Operating System, 2017.
- Valente, Joanna. "The Woman Who Dressed in Gold." *Fleur de Lis*, 2022.

"I Got My Passport Stamped in Hades: Waking the Dead in the Poem" by Leza Cantoral
- Plath, Sylvia. *Ariel*. Faber & Faber, 2015.

"Historical Horror in Poetry" by Sara Tantlinger
- Defoe, Daniel. *A Journal of the Plague Year*: Auroch Press, 2020.
- Larson, Erik. *The Devil in the White City: Murder, Magic, and Madness at the Fair That Changed America*. Vintage, 2004.
- Tantlinger, Sara. *Cradleland of Parasites*. Rooster Republic Press, 2020.
- Tantlinger, Sara. *The Devil's Dreamland: Poetry Inspired by H. H. Holmes*. StrangeHouse Books, 2018.

"Exploring the Monstrous Woman Archetype: Writing *Satan's Sweethearts*" by Marge Simon
- Burkeman, Oliver. "Florida Executes Woman Serial Killer." *The Guardian*, 2002.
- Macdonald, Ross. *The Blue Hammer*. Vintage Crime/Black Lizard, 2008.
- Simon, Marge, and Mary Turzillo. *Satan's Sweethearts*. Weasel Press, 2017.
- Simone, Marge, and Mary Turzillo. *Sweet Poison*. Dark Renaissance Books, 2014.

"Freeing the Demon: Writing Violence Into the Poem" by Claire C. Holland
- Holland, Claire C. "Anna." *I Am Not Your Final Girl: Poems*. GlassPoet Press, 2018.

"Dancing in the Design: Creating Blackout Poetry" by Jessica McHugh
- McHugh, Jessica. *A Complex Accident of Life*. Apokrupha, 2020.
- McHugh, Jessica. *Strange Nests*. Apokrupha, 2022.

"Writing the Wound" by Donna Lynch
- Lynch, Donna. *Choking Back the Devil*. Raw Dog Screaming Press, 2019.

Contributor Bios

Linda D. Addison, HWA Bram Stoker Award® five-time recipient, including *How To Recognize A Demon Has Become Your Friend*. She received the HWA Lifetime Achievement Award, HWA Mentor of the Year and SFPA Grand Master. Her work has made frequent appearances over the years on the honorable mention list for *Year's Best Horror & Best Science-Fiction*. Her site: www.LindaAddisonWriter.com.

Michael Arnzen holds four Bram Stoker Awards® and an International Horror Guild Award for his disturbing (and often funny) poetry, fiction and literary experiments. He has been teaching as a Professor of English in the MFA program in Writing Popular Fiction at Seton Hill University since 1999. Books featuring his horror poetry include Stoker-winners Freakcidents and Proverbs for Monsters, as well as The Gorelets Omnibus from Raw Dog Screaming Press. To see what he's up to now visit gorelets.com or follow him on twitter @MikeArnzen where he routinely posts publishing news, hilarious oddities and random tidbits of terror. For more of his writing advice, see his books, *Instigation: Creative Prompts on the Dark Side* and *Many Genres, One Craft*—or take a course at the HWA's "Horror University" online.

F.J. Bergmann is the poetry editor of *Mobius: The Journal of Social Change*, a past editor of *Star*Line*, the print journal of the Science Fiction & Fantasy Poetry Association, poetry editor for Weird House Press, managing editor for MadHat Press, and freelances as a copy editor and book designer. She lives in Wisconsin and fantasizes about tragedies on or near exoplanets. She was a Writers of the Future winner. Her work has appeared in *Asimov's SF, Polu Texni, Soft Cartel, Spectral Realms, Vastarien*, and elsewhere. While lacking academic literary qualifications, she is kind to those so encumbered. She used to work with horses. She thinks imagination can compensate for anything.

Carina Bissett is a writer, poet, and educator working primarily in the fields of dark fiction and fabulism. Her short fiction and poetry have been published in multiple journals and anthologies including *Upon a Twice Time, Bitter Distillations: An Anthology of Poisonous Tales, Arterial Bloom, Gorgon: Stories of Emergence, Weird Dream Society, Hath No Fury*, and the *HWA Poetry Showcase Vol. V, VI,* and *VIII*. She has also written stories set in shared worlds for RPGs at Green Ronin Publishing and Onyx Path Publishing.

In addition to writing, she has edited several projects; the most recent is in the role as co-editor for *Shadow Atlas: Dark Landscapes of the Americas*. Bissett also teaches generative writing workshops at The Storied Imaginarium and works as a volunteer for the Horror Writers Association (HWA). In 2021, she was acknowledged for her volunteer efforts at HWA with the prestigious Silver Hammer Award. Her work has been nominated for several awards including the Pushcart Prize and the Sundress Publications Best of the Net. She can be found online at http://carinabissett.com.

Leza Cantoral is the Editor-in-Chief of CLASH books, founder of Black Telephone Magazine, and author of *Cartoons in the Suicide Forest* and *Trash Panda*. Born in Mexico, she's a bruja who lives in upstate New York. Find her on Twitter and IG @lezacantoral and at clashbooks.com.

Timons Esaias is a satirist, writer and poet living in Pittsburgh, whose works have been published in twenty-two languages. His story "Norbert and the System" has appeared in a textbook, and in college curricula. Winner of the Winter Anthology Contest, the Louis Award, and (twice) the Asimov's Readers' Award, he was also shortlisted for the 2019 Gregory O'Donoghue International Poetry Prize.

Jeannine Hall Gailey is a poet with multiple sclerosis who served as the 2nd Poet Laureate of Redmond, Washington. She's the author of six books of poetry: *Becoming the Villainess*, *She Returns to the Floating World*, *Unexplained Fevers*, *The Robot Scientist's Daughter*, *Field Guide to the End of the World*, winner of the Moon City Press Book Prize and the Elgin Award, and the upcoming *Flare, Corona* from BOA Editions. She has a B.S. in Biology and M.A. in English from the University of Cincinnati and an MFA from Pacific University. Her work appeared in *The American Poetry Review*, *Ploughshares*, and *Poetry*. Her website is www.webbish6.com. Twitter and Instagram: @webbish6.

Claire C. Holland is a poet and writer from Philadelphia, currently living in Los Angeles. Her first book of poetry, I Am Not Your Final Girl, was nominated for an Elgin Award from the Science Fiction Poetry Association. When she's not writing, she can be found reading romance novels or binge-watching horror movies with her husband and her dog, Chief Brody. She is interested in all forms of art strange and subversive. More about her work can be found at claireholland.com.

James Frederick Leach writes darkly speculative poetry, fiction & drama and is a contributing editor to the website / Youtube channel dailynightmare.com which celebrates Midwest Highbrow Horror. Jim's poetry has been nominated for the Elgin award and his play about John the Baptist won the CITA national playwriting award.

Janice Leach received a Hopwood Award for poetry as an undergraduate and has edited four volumes of Quick Shivers from dailynightmare.com.

Together Jim and Janice are the authors of *Til Death: Marriage Poems* (RDSP, 2017), a collaborative dialogue on the trials and tribulations of sharing a life together. They grow tomatoes near a 100-year-old lilac, listen for ghosts in the midnight, and get up early to discuss each other's dreams. They are currently busy with various schemes botanical, physical, and metaphysical and other writing and poetry projects.

Donna Lynch is a two-time Bram Stoker Award-nominated dark fiction writer, designer, spoken word artist, and the singer and co-founder—along with her husband, artist and musician Steven Archer—of the dark electro-rock band Ego Likeness (Metropolis Records). Her written works include *Isabel Burning*, *Red Horses*, *Driving Through the Desert*; and the poetry collections *In My Mouth*, *Ladies & Other Vicious Creatures*, *Daughters of Lilith*, *Witches*, *Choking Back the Devil*, among others. She is an active member of the Horror Writers Association, and the winner of the 2019 Ladies of Horror Fiction Awards for Best Poetry Collection—*Choking Back the Devil* (Raw Dog Screaming Press). She and her husband live in Maryland.

Alessandro Manzetti (Rome, Italy) is a two-time Bram Stoker Award-winning author, editor, scriptwriter and essayist of horror fiction and dark poetry. His work has been published extensively (more than 40 books) in Italian and English, including novels, short and long fiction, poetry, essays, graphic novels and collections. Website: www.battiago.com.

Jessica McHugh is a novelist, poet, and internationally produced playwright running amok in the fields of horror, sci-fi, young adult, and wherever else her peculiar mind leads. She's had twenty-five books published in thirteen years, including her bizarro romp, *The Green Kangaroos*, her YA series, The Darla Decker Diaries, and her Bram Stoker Award-Nominated blackout poetry collections, *A Complex Accident of Life* and *Strange Nests*. For more info about publications and blackout poetry commissions, please visit McHughniverse.com.

Cynthia Pelayo is an International Latino Book Award winning author and a Bram Stoker Award nominee. She lives in Chicago with her family.

Saba Syed Razvi, PhD is the author of the poetry collections *In the Crocodile Gardens* (an Elgin Award nominee) *heliophobia* (a contender on the preliminary ballot for the Bram Stoker Award® for Superior Achievement in Poetry) as well as the poetry chapbooks *Limerence & Lux; Of the Divining and the Dead*; and *Beside the Muezzin's Call & Beyond the Harem's Veil*. She is currently an Associate Professor of English and Creative Writing at the University of Houston in Victoria, TX, where in addition to working on scholarly research on interfaces between contemporary poetry and science and on gender & sexuality in speculative and horror literature and pop-culture, she is writing new poems and fiction. Learn more at http://www.sabarazvi.com.

Marge Simon lives in Ocala, Florida, with her husband, poet/writer Bruce Boston and the ghosts of two cats. She has three Bram Stoker Awards, Rhysling Awards for Best Long and Best Short Fiction, the Elgin, Dwarf Stars and Strange Horizons Readers' Award. She received HWA's Lifetime Service Award in 2021. Marge's poems and stories have appeared in *Crannog, Bracken, Asimov's, Silver Blade, Journal of Condensed Creative Art, New Myths*, and *Daily Science Fiction*. Her stories also appear in anthologies such as *Tales of the Lake 5, Chiral Mad 4, You, Human*, and *The Beauty of Death*, to name a few. She attends the ICFA annually as a guest poet/writer and is a founding member of the Speculative Literary Foundation. Website: www.margesimon.com

Christina Sng is the three-time Bram Stoker Award-winning author of *A Collection of Nightmares* (2017) and *A Collection of Dreamscapes* (2020) and *Tortured Willows* (2021). Her poetry, fiction, essays, and art appear in numerous venues worldwide, including *Interstellar Flight Magazine, Penumbric, Southwest Review, Weird Tales*, and *The Washington Post*. Visit her at christinasng.com and connect @christinasng.

Lucy A. Snyder is the author of the new poetry collection Exposed Nerves. Nearly 100 of her poems have appeared in publications such as Asimov's Science Fiction, Weirdbook, Vastarien, and Nightmare Magazine. She lives in Columbus, Ohio. Learn more about her at www.lucysnyder.com or follow her on Twitter at @LucyASnyder.

Sara Tantlinger is the author of the Bram Stoker Award-winning The Devil's Dreamland: Poetry Inspired by H.H. Holmes, and the Stoker-nominated works To Be Devoured, Cradleland of Parasites, and Not All Monsters. Along with being a mentor for the HWA Mentorship Program, she is also a co-organizer for the HWA Pittsburgh Chapter. She embraces all things macabre and can be found lurking in graveyards or on Twitter @ SaraTantlinger, at saratantlinger.com and on Instagram @inkychaotics.

Joanna C. Valente is a human who lives in Brooklyn, New York. Joanna is the author of several collections including *A Love Story* and η ψυχή, η ψυχή μας/*the soul, our soul* (forthcoming, Agape Editions). They are the illustrator of *Dead Tongue*, a poetry collection by Bunkong Tuon, and *Raven King*, a poetry collection by Fox Henry Frazier. Joanna received an MFA in writing at Sarah Lawrence College and is also the founder of Yes, Poetry. One day, Joanna dreams of having a flower and vegetable garden.

Albert Wendland is a science-fiction writer and a teacher of fiction-writing at Seton Hill University. He was co-founder of their MFA program in Writing Popular Fiction. His SF novel, *The Man Who Loved Alien Landscapes*, was a starred pick-of-the-week by *Publisher's Weekly*. This was followed by a prequel, *In a Suspect Universe,* and a collection of poems, *Temporary Planets for Transitory Days,* supposedly written by the protagonist of both novels. He's currently working on another book in the same series, and one more will follow. He's also published a study of science fiction, several articles on SF, and a chapter in the writing anthology *Many Genres, One Craft*. He's interested in astronomy, geology, film, graphic novels, landscape photography, and "the sublime."

Bryan Thao Worra is an award-winning Lao poet based in the US who has served two times as the president of the international Science Fiction and Fantasy Poetry Association. He is the first Lao writer to become a professional member of the Horror Writers Association. He has presented at the Smithsonian and represented the nation of Laos during the London 2012 Summer Games as a cultural olympian. He presents regularly on Southeast Asian horror and the Cthulhu mythos. You can visit him online at thaoworra.com.

Editor Bio

Stephanie M. Wytovich is an American poet, novelist, and essayist. Her work has been showcased in numerous magazines and anthologies such as *Weird Tales, Nightmare Magazine, Southwest Review, Year's Best Hardcore Horror: Volume 2, The Best Horror of the Year: Volume 8*, as well as many others.

Wytovich is the Poetry Editor for Raw Dog Screaming Press, and an adjunct at Western Connecticut State University, Southern New Hampshire University, and Point Park University. She is a recipient of the Elizabeth Matchett Stover Memorial Award, the 2021 Ladies of Horror Fiction Writers Grant, and has received the Rocky Wood Memorial Scholarship for non-fiction writing. Wytovich is a member of the Science Fiction Poetry Association, an active member of the Horror Writers Association, and a graduate of Seton Hill University's MFA program for Writing Popular Fiction. Her Bram Stoker Award-winning poetry collection, *Brothel*, earned a home with Raw Dog Screaming Press alongside *Hysteria: A Collection of Madness, Mourning Jewelry, An Exorcism of Angels, Sheet Music to My Acoustic Nightmare,* and most recently, *The Apocalyptic Mannequin.* Her debut novel, *The Eighth*, is published with Dark Regions Press.

Follow Wytovich on her blog at http://stephaniewytovich.blogspot.com, her website at https://www.stephaniemwytovich.com, and on Twitter and Instagram @SWytovich and @thehauntedbookshelf. You can also find her essays, nonfiction, and class offerings on LitReactor.

www.ingramcontent.com/pod-product-compliance
Lightning Source LLC
Chambersburg PA
CBHW022008080426

42733CB00007B/517